Thomistic Papers
IV

Thomistic Papers
IV

Leonard A. Kennedy, C.S.B.
Editor

CENTER FOR THOMISTIC STUDIES
University of St. Thomas
3812 Montrose Boulevard
Houston, Texas 77006

COPYRIGHT © 1988 by
The Center for Thomistic Studies

NIHIL OBSTAT:
Reverend Frank Rossi, S.T.L.
Censor Deputatus

IMPRIMATUR:
Most Reverend Joseph A. Fiorenza
Bishop of Galveston-Houston
December 8, 1987

All rights reserved. No part of this book may be used or reproduced in any manner whatsoever without written permission, except in the case of brief quotations embodied in critical articles or reviews. For information, write to The Center for Thomistic Studies, 3812 Montrose Blvd., Houston, Texas, 77006

LC 83-73623
ISBN 0-268-01867-7 (cloth)
ISBN 0-268-01868-5 (paper)

Manufactured in the United States of America

CONTENTS

Introduction   3
   Leonard A. Kennedy, C.S.B.

Preliminary Statement of Apology, Analysis, and Critique   5
   Henry B. Veatch

A First Incredulous Reaction to Faith and Rationality   65
   Henri DuLac

Adequate Evidence for Religious Assent   73
   Thomas D. Sullivan

Some Considerations concerning Perceptual Practice   101
                 and Christian Practice
   Dennis Q. McInerny

Preliminaries to the Five Ways   129
   Richard J. Connell

Is "God Exists" a Properly Basic Belief?   169
      A Consideration of Alvin Plantinga's Argument
   Joseph Boyle

"Reformed" Epistemology   185
   Thomas A. Russman, O.F.M. Cap.

To

Vernon J. Bourke

Friend and Former Director

of the

Center for Thomistic Studies

and to Janet Bourke

INTRODUCTION

This is the first volume of *Thomistic Papers* which has a unified theme: the rationality of religious belief. All the papers have been written by professors at the Center for Thomistic Studies or at the College of St. Thomas, St. Paul, Minnesota. (Dr. Boyle has now taken a position elsewhere.)

The general stage for discussion is set by Dr. Veatch. Each of the following writers considers one aspect of the discussion. Though there is necessarily some overlap, the matter dealt with is sufficiently important to benefit from a variety of approaches.

It is hoped that this volume will clarify the issues and perhaps help toward a meeting of minds.

Leonard A. Kennedy, C.S.B.

PRELIMINARY STATEMENT OF APOLOGY, ANALYSIS, AND CRITIQUE

Henry B. Veatch

I. Rationality as pertinent to the Faith

A. We begin with the Apology

Thomistic Papers--just what are these anyway? For, although for some years now the three small volumes of such papers have made their periodic appearance under the auspices of the Center for Thomistic Studies at the University of St. Thomas in Houston, it is perhaps to be doubted whether, in the academic profession of philosophy generally, these papers have so much as even been heard of, much less read. After all, significant contributions to Thomistic philosophy are not only in rather short supply these days, but they also, it must be conceded, are scarcely to be numbered among what might be called the really "hot items" in contemporary philosophy. Certainly, they are not in such long supply, nor are they such hot items, as might be contributions to so-called Analytic Philosophy, or to Post-Analytic Philosophy, or to Hermeneutical Philosophy, or to Linguistic Philosophy, or to Deconstruction, or, as Kierkegaard might say, to "astrology and the veterinary sciences or whatever it is that the age demands, all of which are aesthetically and intellectually a huge vulgarity"![1]

Be this, though, as it may, this present volume of *Thomistic Papers* should be noted as having a rather different point and purpose from the earlier ones. For the papers this time are quite consciously polemical in character, all of them being conceived as a rejoinder to an earlier set of essays that were no less polemical, and yet polemical, one might say, to the rather opposite intent. For those earlier essays appeared some four years ago under the title of *Faith and Philosophy*, and under the editorship no less of Alvin Plantinga and Nicholas Wolterstorff.[2] Nor perhaps could one better characterize these two different sets of polemics--first the earlier one, and now this later one--than to say that, while the earlier volume was avowedly counter-Thomistic in its religious and philosophical thrust, this volume seeks to be no less avowedly pro-Thomistic.

"But why?", you might well ask. For are not Thomistic philosophers as eager and interested as others that questions having to do with faith and rationality be once again addressed seriously in these days, and made the object of a properly expert philosophical attention? Particularly, given the near total neglect by professional philosophers, for the greater part of the entire present century, of nearly any and all questions of how philosophy might in any way contribute to the strengthening and better understanding of our Christian religious faith--given such a background, why would not Thomists and Thomist philosophers be among the first to welcome, rather than to rebut, such high quality discussions as those contained in *Faith and Rationality?* Nor is that all. For the editors of *Faith and Rationality*, Alvin Plantinga and Nicholas Wolterstorff, are among America's most competent and outstanding Analytic Philosophers. Why, then, would anyone presume to take on opponents the like of these, least of all a somewhat motley and scattered crew of mere would-be Thomists such as ourselves!

Oh, it's true that neither Plantinga nor Wolterstorff, nor any of their confreres in the project of *Faith and Rationality*, could, by any stretch of reason or imagination, be reckoned as either Catholics in matters of faith, or Thomists in matters of philosophy. Instead, they wear it as their badge of honor (and perhaps even of their divine election) that they are of the Reformed persuasion in religion and of the Analytic persuasion in philosophy. Still, why, for all of that, should we as Thomists want to take on in public debate those who, both professionally and privately, are some of them among our fast friends, Calvinist-Analysts though they be? Besides, when one reads the essays in *Faith and Rationality*, one might almost say--invoking a once fashionable, but now somewhat long-disused terminology--that what these Calvinist-Analysts are about in their cooperative volume resembles nothing quite so much as the once ancient and honorable undertaking of trying to make philosophy serve as the handmaid of theology! And how could Thomists, of all people, object to anything like that?

Or, if "handmaid" be a term that nowadays smacks too much of a reverse discriminatory kind of sexism, why not just say "manservant" instead? In any case, what Plantinga and Wolterstorff and their associates--call them P. W. and Co., if you will--are seeking to do is to put philosophy to use once more as an effective instrument for exhibiting and showing forth the rationality of our Christian faith. Yes, that is the very sense and aim of the title, *Faith and Rationality:* it seeks to point up the fact that the Christian faith is nothing if not rationally respectable, even by today's standards.

Very well, such being the intended purport of *Faith and Rationality*, the question returns once more: what could Thomists possibly find wrong with such a project? To which the answer is that, initially and on the surface, they find nothing wrong with it. The only trouble is that, no sooner do our Calvinist-Analyst friends begin to get down to the details of their own project of seeking to demonstrate the rationality of our Christian faith, than they forthwith cite the case of St. Thomas Aquinas as being the prime example of how *not* to go about any such business as that of a faith seeking understanding. Is it any wonder, then, that, to Thomist readers, the volume *Faith and Ratitionality* should come off as being like nothing quite so much as a throwing down of the gauntlet!

Yes, for what Plantinga, Wolterstorff, and Co. would offer in their volume is a basic reading and interpretation of the entire history of Western religio-philosophical thought from the Middle Ages right down to the present. And what that reading, they think, discloses is that the dominant tradition in that history--at least so far as the business of exhibiting the rationality of our Christian faith is concerned--has been the tradition of so-called "natural theology." Moreover, that same tradition, as P. W. and Co. read it, is a tradition that, both in its origins and in its major articulation, is largely the work of St. Thomas Aquinas. The only trouble is--and here our Calvinist-Analyst friends move to their attack--this entire, elaborate enterprise of natural theology can be shown to have been basically wrong-headed in its origins, and to have now become demonstrably bankrupt in its consequences--no less philosophicaly than theologically. In other words, what P. W. and Co. are concerned to do is to shed a new light on the ancient and honorable tradition of natural theology, a light that will expose it both for its initial wrong-headedness and for its present irrelevance. And where does this new light come from that has thus been vouchsafed to our Calvinist-Analyst antagonists? Well, doubtless they would say that the new light, like all light, must of course come from the Lord. The only thing is that in this case the light from the Lord has not been without mediation. For in theology, they tell us, the light first began to shine forth in the persons of the Reformers in the 16th century, and particularly of their Dutch successors in the ensuing centuries; and in philosophy it would seem that the new light has only recently begun to shine, and this time in the persons of our more brilliant and up-to-the-minute Analytic Philosophers of the present day.

B. The Attack on Natural Theology: the Twin Errors of Evidentialism and Foundationalism

All right, then, as latter-day Thomists, how do we propose to go about defending our master, Thomas, and upholding the honor of his now seemingly largely discredited enterprise of a natural theology? To begin with, though, we still need to get somewhat clearer as to just what it is that is thought to be so wrong with natural theology as this now comes to be seen through the eyes of P. W. and Co. For certainly, insofar as such natural theology has for its aim the exhibition of the rationality of the Christian faith, this objective, so far from being opposed to what the contributors to *Faith and Rationality* have in mind, is an objective that is entirely at one with their own.

Accordingly, it is not so much the objective that St. Thomas and the Thomists have in mind in their project of a natural theology that P. W. and Co. are objecting to, as rather the means and method whereby that objective is supposedly to be carried out. For the way, it would seem, that has been chosen by St. Thomas to carry out this objective is the way of strict logical demonstration--a way that involves a reliance upon self-evident truths at the outset, followed by strict demonstration of such truths as may be demonstrated to follow from the truths that are thus self-evident. Hence, P. W. and Co. take it to be the very hallmark of Thomistic natural theology that in such a theology the attempt is made actually to prove God's existence, as well as to prove that He has certain distinctive attributes--simplicity, unity, goodness, omniscience, omnipotence, *et al.*--all of this supposedly demonstrable in accordance with recognized canons of logical deduction.

In contrast, John Calvin, our Calvinist-Analyst friends remind us, is one who, it seems, just never really concerned himself with all this elaborate logical apparatus of proofs for God's existence and for the divine attributes. Nor did the Reformers generally bother with such things either. It's as if they thought that things of this sort were simply irrelevant, so far as our lives as Christians were concerned. Moreover, when one moves from Reformed theologians to modern and contemporary philosophers, the consensus there seems to be that such proofs are not just irrelevant, but no good. Indeed, ever since Kant, any kind of enterprise that might in any way be thought to be directed toward actually proving the existence of God has been very much under a cloud. Add to this all the new techniques of linguistic and logical analysis that have been developed within Analytic Philosophy in the last several years, and it begins to look as if all of the old proofs and arguments for God's existence not only had not a leg to stand on; in addition, they scarcely seem even to make sense.

Yes, it is the firm consensus of all participants in P. W. and Co.'s enterprise that, if one's concern be that of trying to exhibit the rationality of our Christian faith, resorting to the old proofs for God's existence is just not the way to do it. Yes, one is tempted here to recall Paul Tillich's emphatic and very Germanic outburst of some years ago: "They are not proofs; and it is not Gott!"

Be that as it may, though, one still asks, "But just what is it that is so wrong with this ancient, and one-time honorable, natural-theological enterprise of trying to demonstrate the existence and attributes of God?" To which the specific answer that P. W. and Co. give is that any natural theology of such a sort is vitiated by a twofold fallacy or error--the error of *Foundationalism* and the error of *Evidentialism*.

Nevertheless, to see just what P. W. and Co. mean by these resounding and yet rather opaque terms that serve as their labels for their strictures on natural theology, it might be wise if we were to reproduce, just as a kind of Exhibit A, a highly simplified and even inadequate version of one of the stock arguments that has been put forward as a supposed proof of God's existence.[3] For it is just this sort, or these sorts, of argument that P. W. and Co. would insist are irremediably vitiated by the fact that such arguments, all of them, rely uncritically on the *Foundationalist Principle,* and it is this principle, in turn, that underlies the basic error of Foundationalism that characterizes St. Thomas' entire venture in natural theology. And what, then, is this Foundationalist Principle exactly? Stating it first just in our own terms, it might be said that the principle amounts to little more than one to the effect that if the truth of any proposition is ever to be made evident to us-"rationally evident," as one might say--then it can only be made evident by being *either* seen to be evident just in itself (i.e., self-evident, or *per se notum,* this latter being Thomas' own term for it) *or* by being shown to be derivable from other propositions that themselves ultimately would need to be *per se nota.*[4]

Such, then, is the Foundationalist Principle. And next let us consider briefly just how such a principle comes to be operative in various of the stock arguments or proofs for God's existence. Thus, for example, suppose we develop an argument along the following lines: May it not be taken to be nothing if not self-evident (or *per se notum*) that any being whose existence is contingent cannot be other than a being that is dependent for its existence upon causes outside itself? What's more, should any of these causes of a contingent being's existence--say, of my existence right here and now--be, in turn, dependent upon still other causes for their existence, and these in turn upon still others, then can it be anything but a still further self-evident truth that such a regress of causes could not possibly be a regress *ad infinitum*. For surely, if the regress were infinite, that would mean that, however far one carried the regress back, one would still never have reached the end or terminus of such a series. But, if the regress were thus in itself literally without end, that would mean that, however far back one had traced the regress, one still would not have found sufficient causes to account for even the most petty of contingent facts from which one would have started--e.g., my humble existence right here and now. Accordingly, by the principle of sufficient reason, given that I do in fact exist right here and now, there have to be, concurrently and also right here and now, sufficient causes, or sufficient reasons, to account for this undeniable present existence of mine. Therefore, to obviate such a problem as would be generated by an infinite regress of causes, there has to be an ultimate cause, or an uncaused cause, existing right here and now. Otherwise, there would not be a sufficient reason even for my own puny existence.[5] And, as St. Thomas might have remarked, any such ultimate or uncaused cause "all men would call 'God'."

Surely, we need not bother further with examples and illustrations. For why may we not say that just such a purported proof as the one just cited could suffice as our Exhibit A of how it should be possible to show that our belief in God is indeed a rational belief? So far from God's existence being anything that we simply had to take on faith, it is rather something that we can actually prove and demonstrate--or at least such is the way P. W.

and Co. say that we Thomists view the matter. Not only that, but it should now also be clear how and why such proofs of God and of the divine attributes presuppose the kind of thing that P. W. and Co. call Foundationalism. Thus the Foundationalist Principle specifies that there is no other way in which the truth of a proposition can ever be seen to be rationally evident, unless it be either evident just in itself or else derived from other propositions that are thus immediately evident or self-evident. And so, sure enough, in our Exhibit A, God's existence is made evident in the light of such supposedly self-evident principles as the one to the effect that any being whose existence is contingent must be dependent for its existence on causes outside itself, or the other to the effect that it is impossible for a regress of causes to be infinite.

All right, but now just what is so wrong with all of this? And why, more precisely, do P. W. and Co. seem to think that they need do no more than exhibit or expose this Foundationalist Principle, seemingly so inescapably involved in any and all manifestations of a Thomistic natural theology, in order to condemn such proofs of God's existence simply out of hand?

True, it has been many a long year since proofs of this sort have been at all fashionable in philosophy, or even taken very seriously by anybody any more. And, indeed, the very last thing that one would be likely to hear expounded in the lecture halls of Harvard, or Oxford, or Paris, or really any place else these days, would be anything on the order of the traditional proofs for the existence of God. But, then, so what? For, surely, we may not expect that Calvinist-Analysts as sophisticated as P. W. and Co. would be content merely to dismiss presumed proofs and arguments for God's existence on no other grounds than that they are no longer exactly *à la mode*. For don't we all know that we are here dealing with philosophers, and of course philosophers--particularly Analytic Philosophers--would never allow themselves just to go along with prevailing fashions, merely because they were the fashions? That's the last thing philosophers ever do! Accordingly, why, as but humble and simple-minded and out-of-fashion Thomists, may we not direct a humble petition and advice to our Calvinist-Analyst adversaries, and beg them to at

Preliminary Statement 13

least come out in the open and tell us just what it is that they find to be so wrong with that so-called Foundationalism that in their eyes needs to be taken as the very cornerstone of Thomistic natural theology--a cornerstone which they continually imply is not just crumbling, but already crumbled!

But alas no, there seems to be something about P. W. and Co. such that they cannot seem ever to bring themselves to specify, either too clearly or too fully, just what these criticisms of Foundationalism are, or what the real philosophical grounds for such criticisms might be. Instead, their tactic would seem ever to be one of merely drawing the mantle of their own Analytic sophistication around them, assuming apparently that an attitude of high-minded condescension ought to be able to do duty for anything like considered philosophic criticism. Thus consider the following deliverance by Wolterstorff, right in the very Introduction to *Faith and Rationality:*

> The last decade or so has seen radically new developments in the field of philosophical epistemology. Among the most significant of these developments is the rise of meta-epistemology. Rather than just plunging ahead and developing epistemological theories, philosophers have stood back and reflected seriously on the structural options available to them in their construction of such theories . . . . One of these structural options is classical foundationalism, and most, if not all, philosophers would agree that this option, along with close relatives of it, has constituted the dominant epistemological tradition in the West. What now must be added is that most philosophers who have clearly seen the structure of this particular option have rejected it. On closer scrutiny they have found classical foundationalism untenable.[6]

Alas for us poor Thomists!--or at least for those among us who cannot claim to be members of that exclusive club of latter-day Analysts who have had the good fortune to have been made privy to just what these "new developments" have been in "philosophical epistemology in the last decade or so," which Nick Wolsterstorff would appear to be so taken with, if not even taken in by. True, there are many of us who have read around a bit--yes, some of us even a very great deal--in the epistemological writings of the last decade or so, and yet it would never have occurred to us that any great breakthrough had taken place in epistemology. Rather, we would have supposed it to have been more like a breakdown! But, then, our failures in appreciation of the achievements of recent epistemology may be due to our never before having heard it called by so uplifting a term as "meta-epistemology." That term alone, had we only heard it earlier, might well have caused the scales to fall from our eyes!

C. The Charge of Evidentialism: Is It a Mere Consequence of Foundationalism?

Still, it won't do for us as Thomists to use irony as our only defense. Instead, if P. W. and Co. won't deign to come out and tell us what their much-vaunted meta-epistemological objections are to so-called Foundationalism and the Foundationalist Principle, then we have no alernative but to try to figure out for ourselves just what the hidden moves are in this new meta-epistemology of the Analysts. And, once these moves are actually exposed and brought to light, it should then be possible for us to recognize whether the actual charges leveled against Foundationalism rest rather on misunderstandings, or on faulty reasons, or on just sheer bluff.

Still, this may not be quite the time for us to start beating the bushes and trying to flush out all the hidden meta-epistemological arguments that P. W. and Co. are covertly employing against Foundationalism. Instead, it would seem better were we first to turn our attention to that other charge, which our Calvinist-Analyst friends would seem to want to lay at the door of Thomistic natural theology. This is the charge of so-called Evidentialism.

Preliminary Statement 15

Moreover, the reason we would prefer to look first into this charge, before considering the charge of Foundationalism, is that, as Alvin Plantinga sees things, Evidentialism is a fallacy that is to be regarded as an inevitable consequence of Foundationalism. Hence, in Plantinga's own procedure, he would apparently figure that, if he can first expose some of the enormities of Evidentialism, that should in turn reflect discredit upon the much more basic error, and yet at the same time an error much more difficult to deal with philosophically--viz., the error of Foundationalism.

Accordingly, on our own procedure, let us see if we cannot first show how, so far as Evidentialism is concerned, Plantinga has simply got it wrong: there is just no way in which a thinker like St. Thomas Aquinas could ever rightly be accused of Evidentialism. Yes, one is tempted to wonder whether, in leveling this charge against Aquinas, Al Plantinga may not have been betraying a rather gross ignorance of the relevant texts of St. Thomas, not to mention a curious insensitivity to the really pertinent philosophical and theological considerations. Besides, if it should turn out that the enterprise of natural theology in philosophy does not necessarily lead to any such thing as Evidentialism, so far as our Christian faith is concerned, then Plantinga's effort at poisoning the wells of Foundationalism in advance, and before even examining it, by simply accusing such Foundationalism of generating the error of Evidentialism--this whole clever tactic on Plantinga's part will have been effectively forestalled and aborted.

What, then, is Evidentialism? And just how is it supposed to be the unfortunate spawn and by-product of Foundationalism? Well, already we have noted, more or less in passing, that, so far as Foundationalism and the Foundationalist Principle are concerned, such a principle is nothing if not one having to do with the very rationality of our human beliefs--yes, of any and all human beliefs. For, given any human belief, it would seem always to be in order to raise the question whether any such belief might be said to rest on adequate evidence or not. That is, is the belief a rational one, in the sense of being capable of being justified in terms of truly cogent evidence; or is it a belief for which we must admit that we have but comparatively insufficient evidence, or perhaps no reliable evidence at all?

Moreover, it is just here that Plantinga seeks to invoke the Foundationalist Principle as being relevant to the situation. For what is such a Principle supposed to be, if not the very norm and standard of the rationality or justifiability of any and all beliefs such as we may have? And, further, it is Plantinga's contention that Thomists in general, and St. Thomas in particular, would indeed take the Principle to be just this kind of a norm or standard. Very well, then, that must mean that, if any one of our beliefs should turn out to be either not self-evident in itself, or else not supported by propositions that ultimately are thus self-evident, then that belief must be ruled out as simply irrational and unwarranted.

But, then, what is the import of such a norm or standard, and of the rationality and hence of the acceptability of our beliefs, so far as specifically religious beliefs are concerned? For instance, take our Christian beliefs such as these are enumerated in the Nicene Creed. Can they ever meet the standard of the Foundationalist Principle? Well, so far as the very opening affirmation of the Creed goes, it would seem that, in the eyes of the Thomist, this affirmation might fare very well, as judged by the standards of rationality that are enunciated in the Foundationalist Principle:

> I believe in one God, the Father Almighty,
> maker of heaven and earth, and of all things
> visible and invisible.

Given the apparatus of Thomistic natural theology, and assuming that God's existence, as well as the existence of certain of His attributes, can actually be proved and demonstrated, then it would surely have to be conceded that the acceptance of the first article of the Creed, on the basis of such demonstrations, could not but be adjudged to be other than entirely rational.

But what about the succeeding articles of the Creed--for example:

> And [I believe] in one Lord, Jesus Christ, the only-begotten Son of God; Begotten of the Father before all worlds, God of God, Light of Light, very God of very God; Begotten, not made; Being of one substance with the Father; By whom all things were made, etc.

Clearly, none of these latter beliefs are subject to any rational demonstration in the way in which the belief in God's existence, or in His unity, say, might be subject to demonstration. So what to do?

Well, the usual response of the Christian theologian or philosopher would presumably be simply to admit that all of these subsequent articles of the Creed are to be accepted merely on faith, it being impossible for us (at least in this life) to find or recognize anything like a demonstrative rational evidence of their truth.[7] Nevertheless, as Plantinga sees things, St. Thomas Aquinas could never have been content with this traditional and customary way of viewing the matter. No, for, according to Plantinga, Aquinas insists upon taking the Foundationalist Principle as being the absolute norm or standard of any proper rationality anywhere, be it in matters of science and philosophy, or in matters of religious faith and belief. Hence, for Aquinas, the notion that the acceptance of at least the subsequent articles of the Creed merely on grounds of faith, and not on grounds of reason, could mean that our Christian faith would have to be judged irrational.

But surely, Plantinga thinks, Aquinas would not wish to accept any such consequence as this. And so what is he to do? Well, according to Plantinga, what Aquinas seems to do is to try to dredge up a kind of evidence for the several other articles of the Creed that follow upon the first one. Indeed, Plantinga avers:

> What [Aquinas] means to say is that to believe in the mysteries of the faith is not to be foolish,

or to believe with undue levity, because we have *evidence for* the conclusion that God has proposed them for our belief. This evidence consists in the fulfillment of prophecy and in the signs and wonders accompanying the proclamation of these mysteries.[8]

Now it is by some such means as this, Plantinga thinks, that St. Thomas would attempt to salvage the notion of the rationality, not just of our scientific and philosophical beliefs, but of our religious beliefs as well. In other words, as Plantinga interprets him, Aquinas would extend his Evidentialism so as to cover religious beliefs, no less than properly philosophical or scientific beliefs. Nor is the interesting thing here so much whether Aquinas is successful in thus stretching his Evidentialism to make it cover even our Christian religious beliefs. No, for Plantinga thinks the entire enterprise of Evidentialism is wholly unsuccessful, be it in regard to philosophical beliefs or religious beliefs, either one. After all, Plantinga is convinced that so-called Foundationalism is corrupt, as it were, *per se* and simply in itself, this just not being a proper criterion of rationality either in philosophy or in religion. Hence it is little wonder that Plantinga should think that Evidentialism, as being the unhappy offspring of Foundationalism, should be no less corrupt, particularly when such Evidentialism is made to serve as a criterion for the rational acceptability even of religious beliefs.

Still, the interesting thing just now, we are suggesting, is not whether Aquinas is successful in his purported effort to set up an Evidentialism as being the one true standard of the rational acceptability of our religious beliefs. No, the interesting thing is that, in Plantinga's eyes (at least in this present connection), if St. Thomas can get away with importing his Evidentialism directly into the domain of religious faith, then St. Thomas in effect has radically and profoundly subverted the faith in his very effort to render that faith rational.

For but consider: must not any Christian, be he Orthodox or Roman Catholic, Reformed or Anglican, Lutheran or Zwinglian,

Preliminary Statement   19

Predestinarian or Arminian, or whatever, surely acknowledge that in any true profession of Christianity the believer simply has to accept things on faith, and has to accept them on faith even when there are no reasons, in the proper sense, for his accepting them? Surely, this is nothing if not simply undeniable, so far as religious faith is concerned.

But not so Aquinas--or at least not so Aquinas as Plantinga interprets him. For having committed himself to Evidentialism, Aquinas--so Plantinga thinks--cannot allow himself to admit that even articles of faith are to be accepted without reason, or in the absence of sufficient reasons. That's why, as Plantinga sees it, Aquinas is careful to point out that even the articles of the Creed that follow upon the first article are not things that the Christian is ever to accept without reason. No, for even here one can appeal to such things as miracles, "the fulfillment of prophecy," and "signs and wonders" generally. It is these that can provide us with reasons for our beliefs, and thus spare us having to admit to having anything like purely irrational beliefs.

But, with this, poor St. Thomas would appear to have worked himself into a truly hopeless predicament, so far as anything like a genuine Christian religious faith and commitment on his part is concerned. For, in his determination to secure for the faith an unmistakable and undeniable rationality, he in effect has eliminated anything like faith from Christianity altogether! And surely no Christian, of whatever variety or persuasion, would ever suppose that one could be a Christian without having faith in God and in the Lord Jesus Christ. But does that mean that on Plantinga's analysis St. Thomas turns out not to have really been a Christian at all? Surely, that would be going just a little bit too far--even for Al Plantinga!

D. Aquinas is no Evidentialist--no way!

May we say, then, that perhaps Plantinga is not entirely serious in his insistence that Aquinas was nothing if not a thoroughgoing Evidentialist--an Evidentialist no less in matters of religious faith than in matters of philosophy? Still, notwithstanding, we find that in this connection Wolterstorff even calls John Locke to witness--perhaps a rather anachronistic witness under the circumstances, but still a witness that Wolterstorff does not hesitate to call to testify. Nor is that all, for Wolterstorff is careful to underscore the fact that Locke is nothing if not a typical child of the Enlightenment. Accordingly, Locke insists that any believer who would consider himself to be truly Enlightened--yes, even a Christian believer--would need to be sensitive to his being under obligation to do his utmost always to find adequate reasons and evidence for his religious beliefs. Thus it is that Wolterstorff sums up various of Locke's deliverances on the subject:

> If we are entitled to accept without argument [either that God exists, or] that what God reveals is true, then why may we not also accept without argument that the New Testament, say, is a revelation from God? Because, says Locke, we would then have no way of showing that "the enthusiasts" are irresponsible in their believings.[9]

To this Wolterstorff then adds:

> Of course this challenge to the enthusiasts is also a challenge to Christian believers; if they do not believe on the basis of adequate evidence that the Bible is God's revelation, they too must give up their religion.[10]

Oh, but with quotations to this effect, is it not immediately apparent that P. W. and Co. have surely over-reached themselves? For by no stretch of either the historical or the logical imagination can it ever be imagined that St. Thomas Aquinas in the 13th century was ever a child of the Enlightenment in the 18th century; or that he was in any way or at any time a disciple of John Locke! And, with that, one begins to be suspicious of P. and W.'s entire case to the effect that St. Thomas was even or ever an Evidentialist at all. For one thing, the term "Evidentialist" is itself a term entirely of P. W. and Co.'s own ingenious manufacture, there being no conceivable equivalent to such a thing to be found anywhere in Aquinas.

But then what about Foundationalism? you may ask. For, even though the term Foundationalism is nowhere to be found in Aquinas, surely the sort of thing that is designated by the term would seem to be there. And Foundationalism certainly breeds Evidentialism--that, it would seem, is something that Plantinga would seem almost to stake his very reputation upon. To this, however, the reply simply is that while in a sense St. Thomas might perhaps be said to subscribe to a kind of Foundationalism and also to the Foundationalist Principle--of this we shall have more to say in the succeeding section--it just isn't true that Foundationalism necessarily breeds any kind of Evidentialism. And the reason simply is that St. Thomas never interprets the Foundationalist Principle as being the sole criterion of the rationality of our beliefs, be this either in matters of religious belief or in philosophy. Particularly, Aquinas would never suppose such a principle to operate in the manner of an absolute standard that would bar the acceptance of any belief, be it Christian or otherwise, unless and until the believer had such evidence for his belief as that specified under the terms of the Foundationalist Principle. For there are many things, Aquinas would say, that we come to accept, and accept rationally, on the basis of experience and as a result of induction; and these are far from meeting the criterion of being either self-evident or derivatively evident from that which is thus self-evident.

But let us move on to some specific quotes in evidence of how seriously and even tendentiously P. and W. would appear to have distorted St. Thomas' views. Thus, for example, St. Thomas lays it down as a fundamental principle of all religious faith that "the intellect of the believer assents to that which he believes, not because he sees it [to be true] either in itself, or by resolving it into first principles that are self-evident (*per se visa*), but because he is convinced by divine authority that he should assent to those things which he does not see and on account of the command of his will."[11]

Given pronouncements such as this, how can P. and W. possibly maintain that St. Thomas is precluded from ever supposing that religious truth may be accepted merely on grounds of faith alone? Still more important, it should be noted how St. Thomas makes a seminal and decisive distinction between rational investigation such as may *precede* the act of our will in believing, and such investigations as are prompted by, and thus *follow upon*, what it is our will to believe:

> Human reasoning in support of what we believe may stand in a two-fold relation to the will of the believer. First, as preceding the act of the will, as, for instance when a man either has not the will, or not a prompt will, to believe, unless he be moved thereto by human reason; and in this way human reasoning diminishes the merit of faith . . . . Secondly, human reasons may be consequent to the will of the believer. For, when a man has a will ready to believe, he loves the truth he believes, he thinks out and takes to heart whatever reasons he can find in support thereof; and in this way human reasoning does not exclude the merit of faith, but is a sign of greater merit.[12]

In other words, what Aquinas does in this passage is to provide the very charter and title deed of any proper program of a "faith seeking understanding" (*fides quaerens intellectum*). It is not at all a question of our affirmations of faith and of religious belief having to wait upon a prior authentication by the understanding. Instead, it is a question of faith itself being prior to the understanding and thus being the very guide and inspiration for such eventual and future understanding as we human beings may be able to attain. And surely that puts an effective quietus upon such contentions as both Plantinga and Wolterstooff were at one time given to advancing--viz., that Aquinas is nothing but an Evidentialist, and that as an Evidentialist he cannot avoid conceding that any Christian belief that is based only on faith and not on reason is no better than an irrational belief.[13]

But now, having scotched this snake of Evidentialism, is it not high time--at least in this Preliminary Statement--that we moved on to scotch that other snake of Foundationalism, which P. W. and Co. are so determined operates to invalidate the entire Thomistic account of rationality, much as Evidentialism was supposed to invalidate the Thomistic account of faith. Oh, this is not to say that there is not much more that needs to be said on the question of rationality, precisely in its bearing upon religious faith. For, quite apart from the red herring of Evidentialism, there are any number of other things that P. W. and Co. have to say on the matter of just how and in what way our Christian faith may be said to be properly rational--things which as Thomists we feel need to be examined and criticized. But these are things that may be left to our subsequent essays,[14] and not the sort of thing that should be allowed to clutter up and prolong this already cluttered and overly long Preliminary Statement.

II: Rationality as it Pertains not Just to Religious Belief but to Belief Generally

In the foregoing Part of this Preliminary Statement, our concern was with questions of whether and how "rationality," in the sense of the title "Faith and Rationality," might be understood to have a bearing upon religious "faith." But now with this second Part the issue shifts to that of rationality itself: just what is rationality, and just how may a so-called rational knowledge, or a rational understanding, of things be most properly conceived and understood? Thus, so far as P. W. and Co. are concerned, their thesis in *Faith and Rationality* is that, as a religio-philosophical thinker, St. Thomas Aquinas is sadly confused, and even more sadly confounding, in the account which he gives of the bearing of rationality upon our Christian beliefs; but, still more than that, P. W. and Co.'s really heavy artillery would seem to be directed at St. Thomas' basic notion of human rationality itself, and of the way such rationality functions so as to bring us to something approximating a genuine knowledge and understanding. Moreover, P. W. and Co.'s strategy is first to knock out St. Thomas' very epistemology, and then to install in its place a truly up-dated and sophisticated Calvinist-Analyst version of epistemology--one which will reflect the insights, not to say the blessings, of what Wolterstorff would call the new meta-epistemology.

All right, let us proceed at once to consider the attack on Thomistic epistemology: just how is the attack mounted, and what particular weapons does it use? Already, and even from our earlier discussions, it should be apparent that the focal point of the attack is certain to be directed at what P. W. and Co. like to term the Foundationalism of St. Thomas' epistemological position, and particularly at the Foundationalist Principle upon which that position supposedly rests. Also, as we warned earlier, in trying to counter such attacks on Foundationalism, we poor Thomists find ourselves not a little hampered by the fact that, while P. W. and Co. may not be deliberately masking their batteries, they certainly are not coming clean and telling any mere Thomists what and where these batteries are. Of course, one might say that, so long as we have chosen to speak in the language of battles, and of artillery attacks and counter-attacks, it is scarcely appropriate to complain that our Analyst opponents have not chosen to keep us informed of just what their strategy and tactics are. After all, in any and all war-games, fancied or otherwise, it can hardly be demanded that the language of the game should be other than one of concealment and perhaps even deceit, and thus not one of forthrightness and careful disclosure of argument. But confound the business of language games! And, instead, let us just say that we find it hard not to complain that, in their attack on Foundationalism, our Calvinist-Analyst opponents seem not to deign to let us poor benighted Thomists know just what it is they find to be so mistaken about what they claim is the Foundationalism of St. Thomas, and why they find that Foundationalism to be so wrong-headed philosophically. Instead, they leave it to us simply to guess and make mere surmises as to what their reasons and arguments in the matter really are.

A. Is Foundationalism Self-Referentially Incoherent?

Still, this accusation may not be quite fair, at least not so far as Al Plantinga is concerned. For in the leading essay in the

Preliminary Statement 25

volume, the essay entitled "Reason and Belief in God," he comes right out swinging, and saying precisely why he thinks Thomistic Foundationalism must be repudiated. For the trouble with Foundationalism, Plantinga says, is that it is "self-referentially incoherent." And not only does he say it; he explains just why he says it![15]

All of that notwithstanding, it quickly turns out that, once one begins to scrutinize this charge of Plantinga's more carefully, one begins to wonder whether even he himself would ever have supposed that this particular charge was one to be taken too seriously. Or was it only a kind of diversionary tactic on his part? For no sooner does one consider just how Plantinga chooses to formulate the Foundationalist Principle than one quickly recognizes that, as he formulates it, the Principle certainly is self-referentially incoherent all right. The only trouble is that, formulated that way, the Principle could have not the slightest relevance to Thomistic epistemology at all, with the result that Plantinga's charge of self-referential incoherence is nothing if not just one more red herring!

Recall once more how we ourselves have consistently stated the Principle--viz. that, if any proposition be such that its truth be undeniably evident to us, then that proposition must be seen to be either evident just in itself, or else seen to be derivatively evident from truths that are thus self-evident. And, thus stated, it would indeed seem that the principle purports to be nothing if not itself self-evident; and, as thus purportedly self-evident, the principle as formulated is self-referential. And yet it certainly is in no wise incoherent.

Oddly enough, though, the way in which we have just formulated the Principle is not the way in which Plantinga chooses to formulate it. Instead, he formulates it: for any proposition which is taken to be a "basic proposition," that proposition must be either evident in itself, or else derivatively evident in terms of propositions that are thus self-evident. Moreover, in using the term "basic proposition" Plantinga explains that he means that "a proposition is *basic* for me if I believe it, and do not believe it on the basis of other propositions."[16]

Clearly, though, there is nothing about this way of understanding "basic propositions" that compels one to recognize the Principle, when so formulated, as having to be either self-evident or derivatively evident. Quite the contrary, it is entirely conceivable that I might just accept a proposition as being "basic" for me even though I might well admit that I did not have any decisive evidence of its truth, be it either a self-evidence or a derivative evidence. In contrast, if it be not "basic propositions" in the sense just specified that I am talking about, but rather propositions whose truth I hold to be simply evident to me, then obviously (i.e., self-evidently) under these terms the proposition in question must be either self-evident to me or derivatively evident to me.

Accordingly, formulating the Foundationalist Principle in the way we have done--and that would surely seem to be the normal way of understanding the Principle--then there is no doubt that, as so formulated, the Principle itself is nothing if not self-evidently true; and, as self-evidently true, the Principle may be said to refer to itself in its very formulation. But where, pray tell, could there be any "self-referential incoherence" in such a formulation? In contrast, once the Principle is formulated in the somewhat gratuitous way in which Plantinga chooses to formulate it, then the Principle is in no wise a self-evident truth, and hence to suppose that in its very formulation it refers to itself as being self-evident--this would indeed be patently incoherent.[17]

B. Why Require Self-evident Truths: Are These the Grain or Only the Chaff of Epistemology?

Very well, supposing that P. W. and Co.'s first and really only ostensible criticism of the Foundationalist Principle--viz., that it is self-referentially incoherent--is a criticism that is lacking, alike in cogency and in relevance, what now of their other and more covert criticisms? And here first of all--as one might very well suspect--P. W. and Co. are inclined to take a rather dim view

Preliminary Statement

of the whole idea of so-called self-evident principles as ever being able to serve as proper principles for a genuine human knowledge. This is not to say, of course, that P. W. and Co. would simply deny outright that there are any self-evident truths. Quite the contrary, Plantinga insists that self-evident truths are one kind of "basic propositions," as he puts it. Moreover, as he defines basic propositions, these are propositions that are rationally acceptable, even though their acceptance be not based on the acceptance of any other prior propositions from which the former might be derived. And, certainly, self-evident propositions unquestionably meet this criterion of being basic.

On the other hand, even though P. W. and Co. are quite willing to accept self-evident propositions as being basic, they are equally given to implying, if not actually asserting, that self-evident propositions amount to little more than purely logical or linguistic truths, which are for that reason wholly uninformative. Or at least they are uninformative in the sense of being unable to yield any information about facts in the world.

Still, we need to consider some of the examples which Plantinga himself gives of such self-evident truths.[18] For instance:

(1) $2 + 1 = 3$

or

(2) No man is both married and unmarried.

Likewise, there are various truths of logic, as they might be called, which Plantinga also takes to be self-evident:

(3) For any proposition p the conjunction of p with its denial is false.

(4) If p is necessarily true and p entails q, then q is necessarily true.

(5) The proposition *all men are mortal* is distinct from the proposition *all mortals are men*.

And, finally, Plantinga adds still further examples such as:

(6) The whole is greater than the part.

And, rather "more dubiously," as Plantinga remarks, a proposition such as:

(7) Man is an animal.

No sooner, though, does one consider propositions such as these, that Plantinga cites as being examples of self-evident truths, than anyone--particularly among present-day philosophers--will no doubt be struck by what nearly everyone will take to be the common feature or character of such propositions. For are they not all of them in the nature of what might be called purely verbal or linguistic truths? In any case, they are certainly not "truths about the world," as the current saying goes. Nor are they truths that would seem to be derived from experience and observation as, for example, a proposition like "Silver melts at 960.5° C" would be. Yet, despite this non-factual, non-empirical character of these self-evident truths, would it not seem that, if we are to heed the requirements of the Foundationalist Principle, it must be just such presumably empty and hollow truths as these self-evident truths that have to be reckoned as being no less than basic principles upon which any and all genuine human knowledge must needs be erected? For does not the principle stipulate that the only way in which the truth of any proposition can be made evident to us is either by its being seen to be evident just in itself, or else by its being seen to be derivable from other truths that are thus self-evident?

Is it any wonder, then, that P. W. and Co. are inclined to think that "something is rotten in Denmark" with the Foundationalist Principle? That principle, they say, has simply got to go, if one is ever to give any proper account of human rationality and human knowledge and understanding. And the

Preliminary Statement   29

reason it has got to go is that it presupposes that all genuine human knowledge--yes, all human rationality--must ultimately be but an affair of quite empty self-evident truths, or at least be reducible to such truths. All the same, be it noted that, while P. W. and Co. repudiate the notion of self-evident principles playing the role in knowledge that the Foundationalist Principle requires that they play, that certainly does not mean that P. W. and Co. deny that there are self-evident truths. Far from it. Thus, for example, in Plantinga's very notion of "basic propositions," which we alluded to in the foregoing section, Plantinga would classify self-evident truths as one kind of "basic propositions." And indeed there is no denying that a self-evident truth certainly meets Plantinga's criterion of a basic proposition, for self-evident truths certainly are not the kind of truths that one ever believes on the basis of other propositions.

Very well, then, let us say that P. W. and Co.'s objection to self-evident truths is neither that there are no such things, nor that they are not "basic propositions." Instead, their only objection is that, rather than having the decisive role in human knowledge that the Foundationalist Principle requires that they have, they need be relegated to the mere sidelines of human knowledge and understanding.

All the same, could it be that P. W. and Co. may have moved a bit too far, too fast, in their dismissal of self-evident truths? For consider the following propositions:

(8) Silver melts at 960.5° C.

or

(9) Ontogeny recapitulates phylogeny.

Clearly, these are not self-evident propositions. Nor presumably would they be examples of what P. W. and Co. would call "basic propositions." For certainly both (8) and (9) are based on other propositions, being, let us suppose, both of them, but inductive generalizations based on propositional reports of observations and experiments. Nevertheless, let us for a minute stop to cosider if (8) and (9) might not seem, at least superficially, rather like proposition (7) above, which for our present purposes we will simply render as "All men are animals." Would not (7) appear to be no less a truth about the world than (8) and (9)? And likewise could (7) not be said to be a truth that human beings could be said to have learned from experience? For why is it anything other than simply a truth of fact, and a truth of fact derived from our human experience, that has come to be borne in upon us, and as a result of which we have been brought to recognize that animality and rationality are nothing if not distinguishing features of human beings?

Yet note that Plantinga does not think so. Indeed, may we not guess that that was just why it was that, when he cited (7) as one of his examples, he added immediately that it was a somewhat more "dubious"[19] example of a self-evident truth than were his other examples (1)-(6)? Nor is it hard to guess why he regards this example as a dubious one: it is because, (7) being regarded as a self-evident truth, Plantinga then is determined that it not be taken as a truth about the world, or as a truth based on experience. In fact, if we should take it to be a truth of the latter sort, then Plantinga, as it would seem, just dogmatically rules that it cannot be a self-evident truth, it being no less a dogma with him that a self-evident truth can never be anything more than purely verbal or linguistic in character--as if, for instance, men could be said to be self-evidently or necessarily animals on no other ground than that the word "animal," just by its very meaning, is bound up with or implicated in the meaning of the mere word "man."[20]

From this, though, one can immediately guess that Plantinga's way of understanding "self-evident truths" is radically different from the way Aquinas would understand them, or similarly from the way in which Aristotle might be presumed to have understood a notion such as that of propositions that are *per se nota*. Oh, it's true that none of the propositions (1)-(7) would either Aristotle or Aquinas have denied were self-evident. And yet the more likely sorts of examples that Aristotle or Aquinas would have given of such truths as were *per se nota* would have been truths like (7);

Preliminary Statement 31

and indeed for them (7) would be reckoned as *per se notum* for the very reason that Plantinga would deny that it was so--viz., that it is a self-evident truth about the world, and one that is derived from our experience of the world.

Or, again, consider such principles and propositions as play very decisive roles in Aristotle's physics or metaphysics, e.g.:

(10) No accidents but what they are accidents of substances.

(11) Any change that occurs in the world cannot be anything other than a change *of* something, *from* that thing's being something, *to* its being something else.

Clearly, in judgments such as these--at least so they would be in the eyes of Aristotelians and Thomists--(10) and (11) clearly report what is true of the world of nature as we human beings know it from our experience. True, the judgment that a quality or a quantity or an action has to be the quality or the quantity or the action of something is a necessary truth, or a truth *per se notum*, in a way in which (8) (Silver melts at 960.5° C) certainly is not, this latter being, one might say, but an inductive generalization from experience. And yet the fact that one could not conceivably have an instance of an action such as walking without there being anything that was doing the walking, whereas in contrast it is quite conceivable that on a given occasion silver might not melt at the particular temperature predicted--all of this does not mean that the one truth any more than the other is not about the world or is not learned from experience.

Very well, then, suppose that Plantinga, no less than Aristotle and Aquinas, would all of them admit that there are such things as self-evident truths, still it should now be apparent from the examples we have given that the Moderns have come to regard such truths in a very different way from the Ancients. In fact, there has been nothing less than a veritable sea-change in the way in which such truths once tended to be construed by someone like Aquinas, and the way in which a present-day Analyst like Plantinga would construe them. Nor could the difference be summed up any better than to say that it is simply a difference between, on the one hand, regarding self-evident truths as basic and fundamental to any rational understanding that we human beings might be able to attain with respect to the nature of the world and of reality; and, in contrast and on the other hand, going along with the widespread latter-day consensus that such self-evident truths are never more than trivial, and have no bearing whatsoever on the world of experience, being wholly *a priori* and verbal and without relevance, so far as conveying any real information about the facts is concerned.

Nor is it hard to account for this sea-change in the way in which self-evident truths were regarded in the older philosophical tradition, and have now come to be regarded in the tradition that prevails today. For, to put it somewhat briefly and summarily: in modern times such supposed self-evident truths have had to undergo a veritable dousing in an acid bath, first by the Cartesians, and then later by the Kantians. Nor is it hard for one to picture to oneself how these poor self-evident truths must have fared, once they were passed through a cleansing of Cartesian clear and distinct ideas. For was it not ever Descartes' counsel--or rather his requirement--that nothing be accepted as true save only that which we can conceive clearly and distinctly? Moreover, that which is conceived thus clearly and distinctly, Descartes would have said, could not be anything other than what is self-evident and *per se notum*, or else derived therefrom logically. But it is little wonder that, uncompromising Rationalist that he was, Descartes should have immediately gone on to decree that any such self-evidence in matters of truth could not be other than an evidence of pure reason, and hence in no wise an evidence of the senses at all. And so it was, then, that self-evident truths came to be pronounced purely *a priori* truths; and doubtless so indeed they did become, once they had gone through the Rationalist acid-bath of Cartesian fashioning. But that this should have also involved a veritable sea-change from the way in which such self-evident truths had been regarded by Aristotle and Aquinas goes without saying.

With this, though, we need to take still another step forward in the history of Western philosophy--or shall we call it a "great leap forward"? Or even more appropriate might it be to call it "one step forward, and two steps back"! In any case, our step this time leads us into the by now supposedly rather well-charted wilderness of Kantian philosophy, and more particularly to Kant's determination simply to treat all self-evident truths as "analytic truths." Again, and with apologies for a certain over-simplification, would it be incorrect to say that the kinds of truth that Aquinas regarded as being *per se nota*, as well as the *a priori* truths of Cartesian coinage--these all now come to be treated by Kant as no more than Analytic Truths? Further, as we all know, Kant insisted that his Analytic Truths were not to be construed as being in any wise truths about the world. Instead, one might say that they amount to little more than truisms, or what later came to be known as mere linguistic truths. Nor would it seem scarcely deniable that one can hardly pretend to learn very much about the world from such patently self-evident truths as "A bachelor is an unmarried man," or even Kant's own example (but taking it in the way Kant construed it), "All bodies are extended."[21]

And so returning, then, to Al Plantinga and his Calvinist-Analyst cohorts, as well as to that conception of theirs of self-evident truths, that we found to be so different from Aquinas' conception, may we not now see that Plantinga's conception of self-evident truths simply reflects that long and dubious heritage which present-day Analytic Philosophy has arrogated to itself from Descartes and from Kant? Self-evident truths, in short, are nowadays conceived, for the most part quite uncritically, as we would think, as being purely *a priori* truths, and not based on experience at all; and, likewise, they are conceived as being truths that are little more than purely verbal and, for that reason, as not in any way informative as regards things in the world at all.

Moreover, given this kind of a conception of self-evident truths, we can now begin to see just why P. W. and Co. would be so dismissive of the Foundationalist Principle, and more generally of that Foundationalism which in their eyes is at the very core of any Thomistic epistemology. For one thing, as P. W. and Co.

see things, the Foundationalist Principle is regarded by Thomists as being no less than the absolute norm or standard of any and all truth such as is based on any kind of proper evidence, and hence as no less than the very criterion of rationality itself and of all rational knowledge. Accordingly, for Thomists, as P. W. and Co. interpret them, it would seem that all true knowledge would have to be couched either in self-evident propositions or else in such propositions as could be derived by logical deduction, and presumably even *more geometrico,* from original self-evident propositions.

Nevertheless, right at this point, we feel that we must interrupt for but a moment the main line of our present exposition and argument, in order to interject a brief parenthesis by way of protest. For be it noted that nothing could be a more gross distortion of the Thomistic view of knowledge than the sort of absolutizing of the Foundationalist Principle, which P. W. and Co. would appear to want to foist upon the Thomists. For, while it is true that, doubtless in St. Thomas' eyes, any proposition whose truth is fully evident to us must be a proposition that is either self-evident or at least derived from truths that are self-evident, still St. Thomas would be the first to warn against the sort of Rationalist epistemological optimism of which someone like Descartes would seem guilty. No, for it is a fundamental consideration with both Aristotle and Aquinas that all human knowledge must arise in and from experience; and, while it is sometimes the case, as, for example, with propositions like (10) and (11), that the knowledge that is prompted by our human experience turns out to be a knowledge that is no less than an evident knowledge (i.e., its truth is rationally evident to us), this is but rarely the case and, even when it is the case, it is the case, as it were, only precariously. Hence, whatever may be the goal or the ideal of human knowledge as this proceeds from experience, in fact most of the knowledge that we are able to achieve turns out to be no more than a mere inductive knowledge, and hence not a knowledge in the sense of a fully evident knowledge, not to mention a full and complete knowledge. After all, such a perfection of knowledge just isn't for us human beings, at least not in this life. Instead, here we "see through a glass darkly," and only then "face to face" (*I Corinthians*, 13:12). Accordingly, while a self-evident knowledge may well be the goal of human knowledge, it is but very occasionally that any self-evident truths are attained by us at all; and, even in regard to these few, it is not infrequently that we are deceived even as to their supposed self-evidence. There is just no denying that the roadway of human knowledge is strewn with the wreckage of supposed self-evident truths.

But, this parenthesis and protest aside, and returning to P. W. and Co. and their understanding of the Foundationalist Principle, it should be possible now better to understand why such a principle, considered as a basic principle of human rationality, should strike them as being anathema. And little wonder! For, if self-evidence is to be understood to be what it is only after having been put through the Cartesian and the Kantian acid bath, then no self-evident truth could ever have any basis in experience or really be in any way empirically relevant; and likewise no self-evident truth could ever be in the least informative as regards the facts, or the world, or reality, or whatever. Nor is that all for, just as that self-evidence of truth which the Foundationalist Principle would appear to demand amounts to little more than a sort of cognitive fraud, so also the deducibility of truths from self-evident principles, which the second part of the Foundationalist Principle would seem to demand--this also P. W. and Co. would see as being fraudulent as well. For but consider: if self-evident truths, on the Kantian analysis, are always and invariably to be reckoned as uninformative, and if, in any deductive logical demonstration, there can be no more information in the conclusion of a demonstration than is already contained implicitly in the premises, then it would seem that no one could ever hope really to learn anything from logical demonstrations--at least not from such demonstrations as are sanctioned by the Foundationalist Principle.

And so once again--on that Principle--at least as it would seem to be interpreted by P. W. and Co., any knowledge that, in the sense of the Principle, is rationally evident must be a knowledge whose truth is either self-evident, or derivatively evident in the light of other and prior truths that are self-evident.

And so is it any wonder that against this background, and interpreting the Foundationalist Principle in the more or less Cartesian and Kantian contexts that we are suggesting that P. W. and Co. are inclined to do, the upshot will be that P. W. and Co. will think that the Foundationalist Principle is not just irrelevant, but even subversive of all genuine knowledge, and needs to be eliminated, root and branch? And similarly, is it any wonder that, having so uncritically equated Thomistic epistemology with a total commitment to so utterly discredited a version of Foundationalism, P. W. and Co. should think that Thomism and Thomistic rationality need to be simply written off as but a philosophical snare and delusion! And so it should be, if P. W. and Co. are right about what they say Thomistic rationality involves. But of course, they aren't right--at least not about that!

C. Why Not Basic Propositions Instead of Self-evident Truths?

Before, however, we turn to the business of trying to rehabilitate the Thomistic notion of rationality in the face of the misplaced strictures of P. W. and Co., we need first to have a look at what that notion of rationality and of a properly rational knowledge is that P. W. and Co. would want to advocate in place of a Thomistic kind of Foundationalism. Thus what about the proposition "God exists"? What do they say as to the rationality of such a belief? After all, P. W. and Co. not only say that they do indeed believe in God's existence, but they are no less determined to argue that such a belief is entirely rational--i.e., their belief is not a case of mere Fideism,[22] in which the proposition "God exists" is said to be accepted solely on faith, and not as a rationally defensible truth. But, then, how do P. W. and Co. defend the rationality of this belief of theirs in God's existence? Clearly, in view of all the water that has flowed over the dam in this paper of ours thus far, we can be in no doubt that the very last thing P. W. and Co. will try to do by way of exhibiting the rationality of their belief in God will be to try in any way to prove or demonstrate the truth of the proposition "God exists." No, for demonstrations conceived in the spirit of the Foundationalist Principle are simply out! But what, then, is the alternative? For obviously "God exists" is not a proposition which P. W. and Co.

would take as being in any way self-evident; and, even if they did so take it, we have seen how, in their eyes, self-evident truths being uninformative, the self-evidence of "God exists" would not convey the slightest knowledge of whether God really existed or not.

So what, then, is the ploy which P. W. and Co. propose to us by way of exhibiting the rationality of the belief that God exists? Immediately, Plantinga's answer to this question--and we take it that his answer is definitive for the other contributors to *Faith and Rationality*--is that "God exists" is simply "a basic proposition," that term being a technical term in the Plantinga epistemology. What, then, does the term mean? It means simply that a "basic proposition" is one whose truth is not based on any other proposition. That is to say, its truth cannot be said to be in any way evidenced by any other truths, or to be in any way based on any reasons or arguments, or demonstrations, or any other kind of external evidence whatever.

"Oh," but one might say, "if a basic proposition is one whose truth is not based on any external evidence, must that not mean that its truth must therefore be somehow self-evident?" "But no," Plantinga would say, "that is not the only alternative." True, he would grant that there are self-evident propositions, and that these could properly be taken to be examples of "basic propositions," inasmuch as the truth of any basic propositions certainly is not derived from or based on any other proposition. Still, the basicality of a proposition like "God exits" is not like the basicality of self-evident truths: for one thing, and most decisively, self-evident truths are non-informative, whereas "God exists" is, for P. W. and Co., not just informative, but crucially so!

Very well, then, let's consider another class of examples that Plantinga would give of basic propositions, a class of propositions quite different from self-evident propositions. These are just ordinary empirical or factual assertions such as:

(12) There is a tree before me.

(13) I am wearing shoes.

(14) That tree's leaves are yellow.

Now in just what sense are such ordinary empirical assertions to be reckoned as basic propositions? Well, Plantinga seems to say they are basic just in the sense that they are directly evident to the senses, and evident to the senses precisely in the sense that they are not derived from, or based upon, any other evidence than simply the very perception or observation itself. For example, in (13), I just see that I am wearing shoes. That's why it is both true and a basic proposition.

All right, then, what about "God exists"? Is that a basic proposition in the way in which (13), "I am wearing shoes," is? Well, hardly, for Plantinga would presumably not say that God's existence is evident to me in the way in which the fact that I am wearing shoes is evident--i.e., I just look and perceive I am wearing shoes. No, this is not at all what Plantinga would say: I do not have merely to look and I will see. All the same, Plantinga does insist that, even though "God exists" is neither self-evident nor evident to the senses, it is a basic proposition for all of that, in that it is not asserted on the basis of any other proposition. Not only that but, inasmuch as it is a basic proposition, it would seem that I am entirely rational in thus asserting that God exists. Yes, I am altogether "within my epistemic rights," as P. sometimes likes to put it, in so affirming that God exists.

But how so? For does this not seem to smack almost of paradox? Thus, by Al Plantinga's own account of the matter, it would appear that we could, in a quite specific sense, have no reason for asserting that God exists. For, "God exists" being basic, it is not based on any other proposition, or propositions, of any kind, be they empirical propositions or otherwise: it is neither deduced from them, nor induced from them, nor in any way derived from them, nor dependent upon them for any conceivable kind of evidencing that might be provided for that proposition's truth. How then could it possibly be said to be rational for us to accept that proposition even when we have no evidence for it, and therefore no reason or reasons of any kind for believing it? Surely, Al Plantinga is not trying to tell us, is he, that it is the very absence of any reasons for accepting such basic propositions that has to be the thing that gives us a reason for accepting them? Putting it that way would be not just logically odd, but downright dumbfounding!

Suppose, though, we try a somewhat different tack in our effort to make some sense out of Plantinga's confident assertion that we have every reason to believe a basic proposition such as "God exists"--and this even though, in another sense (or is it the same sense?), we have no reason for believing it. For it may be that there is another class of basic propositions, other than self-evident propositions, and also other than propositions that in the usual sense are simply evident to the senses. Perhaps, then, "God exists" will turn out to be a basic proposition of this somewhat different kind or class. And, sure enough, Plantinga in his examples of basic propositions would seem to classify the assertion "God exists" more or less with assertions to the effect that there are physical objects, or that there are other minds.[23] For instance, take the belief in other minds. Seemingly, this is a case in which we could hardly be said to have any direct perception of another person's mind. For, even though I might quite properly be said to observe my neighbor going through all sorts of bodily writhings and contortions of his facial muscles, etc., I can hardly say that I actually see or observe his pain. Or, again, in the matter of so-called physical object statements, I certainly have direct perceptual evidence of colors, shapes, sizes, yes, even of motions; but, strictly speaking, the physical objects that have these colors, or are of these sizes, or are in motion, I do not perceive as such--or at least not directly.

But, then, is the case one of my inferring the existence of physical objects from the perception of their sense data, or of my inferring the existence of other minds from the perception of people's writhings and contorting of themselves in a highly indicative manner? Once more, the answer has to be "No." For, basic propositions being basic, they cannot be said to be inferred from reasons, or, indeed, from other evidence of any kind. To which the only answer would seem to be, "Bravo!" For one simply has to hand it to Plantinga for being as courageous as he is consistent! The only trouble is that, for all of his courage and consistency, Plantinga seems to leave us with little more than sheer paradox, so far as his theory of basic propositions is concerned. For but consider: we are rationally justified, Plantinga assures us, in believing in such things as the existence of physical objects, of other minds, and of God. All the same, none of these beliefs is justified on the ground of being either self-evident or empirically evident. And, if we then ask whether such beliefs may be considered rational beliefs on the ground that they are somehow inferrable from beliefs that are either empirically evident or perhaps self-evident, Plantinga throws up his hands in horror and exclaims: "But to suppose that the truth of such basic propositions is based on inference is to violate their very charter as basic propositions, since by definition no *basic* proposition can be in any way based on, or derived from, any other proposition!"

What, then, are we to say? For seemingly, in his account of basic propositions as being propositions which we are entirely rational in believing, we are precluded by the rules of the basic-proposition game from having any reason to believe them. Surely, this sounds as if Plantinga wanted to have his cake and eat it too![24]

D. What About Causes Instead of Reasons for our Rational Beliefs?

Let it not be thought, though, that P. W. and Co. are entirely without resource, even when they would thus seem to be caught out in the business of both wanting to have their cake and eat it too. And so let us quickly look at their new and latest resource that they would now resort to. Thus the question, or challenge, that P. W. and Co. are seeking to answer at this juncture is just the question as to what possible grounds Al Plantinga can have for insisting that we human beings have "a right"--Plantinga calls it an "epistemic right"--simply to affirm propositions of the character of "There are physical objects," "There are other minds," and "God exists." Moreover, the fact that we have an epistemic right to make such assertions means, so Plantinga would also insist, that we are entirely rational in doing so. But why and on what grounds is Plantinga able to say this? Could it be that Plantinga's contention as to the "rightfulness" and the "rationality" of our making assertions of this kind--i.e., of the existence of physical objects, or of other minds, or of God--are due simply to the fact that, as one might say, "everyone does it," or "we all do it." And, indeed, is it not true that we all of us do unhesitatingly and daily affirm that there are physical objects, and that there are other minds? Not only that, but may it not also be said that we cannot very well help making assertions or affirmations of this sort? Indeed, would we not think that no one other than a madman could consistently refuse to believe that there were any physical objects or that other people had any minds or feelings? In other words, we just can't help believing that there are other minds, or that there are physical objects.[25]

With that, however, the question comes round to being one of whether the mere fact that we all of us feel impelled, or even compelled, to make assertions to the effect that there are physical objects, or are other minds, implies that the rationality of such assertions is thereby assured. Indeed, if such be the character of Plantinga's argument for the rationality of his so-called "basic propositions," it might just occur to one that this sounds not unlike Hume's appeal to custom as being the explanation for our inescapable human tendency to move from "constant conjunction" to "necessary connection." And yet would not Hume be the first to say that, while our experience of constant conjunction might be the *cause* of our being convinced that necessary connection was involved, it certainly could in no wise be said to constitute a proper *reason* in justification of our affirmation of such necessary connection? But does that then mean that Al Plantinga has been guilty of an elementary confusion of causes with reasons in this matter of the supposed ground or basis for the rationality of basic propositions?[26]

Accordingly, having raised this kind of difficulty with respect to Plantinga's account of the rationality of our affirmations of physical object statements, or statements about other minds, what about an affirmation to the effect that God exists? For this, after all, is the decisive sort of example that Plantinga must deal with in his concern to establish the rationality of our assertions of basic propositions even when we have no reasons or evidence for the truth of such propositions. How, then, can Plantinga explain and defend his contention that it is perfectly rational for one to assert that God exists, even when it is admitted that that proposition is neither self-evident, nor empirically evident, nor in any way derivatively or demonstrably evident either? True, Plantinga does suggest that such an affirmation of God's existence is on all fours with affirmations like those of the existence of physical objects or of other minds so that, if the latter sorts of affirmation are rational, so is the former. And yet that is just the question: How can one maintain that the affirmation of any of these so-called basic propositions is ever rational? After all, so far as propositions about physical objects or other minds are concerned, all Plantinga seems able to come up with is the notion that there presumably are causes--perhaps psychological causes--that would account for our making such assertions. And yet causes are not reasons. So what about a proposition, then, like "God exists"?

This time Plantinga seems inclined to respond by quoting a presumably somewhat eloquent passage from John Calvin in his support:

> There is within the human mind, and indeed by natural instinct, an awareness of divinity. This we take to be beyond controversy. To prevent anyone from taking refuge in the pretense of ignorance, God himself has implanted in all men a certain understanding of his divine majesty. Ever renewing its memory, he repeatedly sheds fresh drops. Since, therefore, men one and all perceive that there is a God and that he is their maker, they are condemned by their own testimony because they have failed to honor him and to consecrate their lives to his will. If ignorance of God is to be looked for anywhere, surely one is most likely to find an example of it

among the more backward folk and those more remote from civilization. Yet there is, as the eminent pagan says, no nation so barbarous, no people so savage, that they have not a deep-seated conviction that there is a God. So deeply does the common conception occupy the mind of all, so tenaciously does it inhere in the hearts of all! Therefore, since from the beginning of the world there has been no region, no city, in short no household, that could do without religion, there lies in this a tacit confession of a sense of deity inscribed in the hearts of all.

Indeed, the perversity of the impious, who though they struggle furiously are unable to extricate themselves from the fear of God, is abundant testimony that this conviction, namely, that there is some God, is naturally inborn in all, and is fixed within, as it were in the very marrow. . . . From this we conclude *that it is not a doctrine that must first be learned in school,* but one of which each of us is master from his mother's womb and which nature itself permits no one to forget.[27]

And, immediately, Plantinga's comment on this passage is:

Calvin's claim, then, is that God has created us in such a way that we have a strong tendency or inclination toward belief in him. . . . The fact is, Calvin thinks, one who does not believe in God is in an epistemologically substandard position--rather like a man who does not believe that his wife exists, or thinks she is like a cleverly constructed robot and has no thoughts, feelings, or consciousness.[28]

Somehow, when one reads this passage from Calvin as quoted by Plantinga, it is hard not to be struck with utter astonishment--not astonishment at how someone like Calvin might have written such a passage, but rather astonishment at how and why someone like Plantinga should think that he can quote such a passage to the purpose he does. For his purpose is to show that the acceptance of basic propositions--and specifically, this time, of the proposition that God exists--is properly rational, even when there is no rational evidence in support of the proposition. Why, then, do we accept the proposition? Well, presumably it is because God has implanted it "in the hearts of all," it is just "naturally inborn in all," it is in us in fact by "a natural instinct." Surely, though, these are all only in the nature of *causes* of our believing in God and not *reasons* for our doing so. Yet, on the next to the last page of his essay in *Faith and Rationality,* Plantinga unabashedly asserts: "Belief in the existence of God is in the same boat as belief in other minds, the past, perceptual objects; in each case *God has so constructed us* that in the right circumstances we form the belief in question."[29] And then Plantinga confidently concludes: "But then belief that there is such a person as God is as much among the deliverances of reason as those other beliefs."[30]

And yet does this conclusion really follow from the argument Plantinga would appear to have adduced in its support? For, remember, it is not the mere fact that the affirmation of God's existence is like, or analogous to, such other affirmations as that other minds exist, or that past events have taken place, or that physical objects exist--no, it is not the mere analogy between an affirmation of God's existence and such other affirmations that warrant their being reckoned as "deliverances of reason." Rather, it is the fact that all of us human beings are "so constructed" that we cannot do other than make such affirmations--that presumably is the factor in the situation that is supposed to render such propositions rationally acceptable to us. Surely, though, this will never do! For does it not involve once again a patent confusion of causes for a belief with reasons for that belief? And, surely, if we are lacking reasons for a belief, it is hard to see how something like a mere conditioned affirmation of such a belief could ever render it a "deliverance of reason."

Perhaps, though, we still need rather more by way of evidence and argument in support of this contention of ours that, in his presumed confounding of mere causes for our beliefs with reasons for our beliefs, Plantinga would seem to have committed nothing if not an enormous howler. Accordingly, let us invoke a somewhat amusing example that R. M. Hare resorted to a number of years ago, by way of bringing it home--albeit to a somewhat different point and purpose from our own--just why and how causes for a belief ought not to be confused with reasons for a belief:

> A certain lunatic is convinced that all dons want to murder him. His friends introduce him to all the mildest and most respectable dons that they can find and, after each of them has retired, they say, "You see, he doesn't really want to murder you; he spoke to you in a most cordial manner; surely you are convinced now?" But the lunatic replies "Yes, but that was only his diabolical cunning; he's really plotting against me the whole time, like the rest of them; I know it, I tell you." However many kindly dons are produced, the reaction is still the same.[31]

Do we need then even to bother to point the moral of this quotation, so far as Plantinga is concerned? Put very simply, the moral is none other than that, for all of there having been presumably no lack of causes for the poor lunatic's belief that all Oxford dons were out to murder him--after all, a psychologist or psychiatrist could no doubt have produced any number of such causes in a diagnosis of the man's lunacy--that still does not mean that the lunatic had anything like good reasons or sound evidence for his belief that all dons were determined to murder him. And so with Plantinga: it does not suffice merely to adduce causes for our beliefs, if what one wants to do is to establish that we have good reasons for our beliefs.

E. Why Not Reliable Beliefs Rather Than True Beliefs?

But no, Plantinga is still not dead yet--far from it! And, indeed, just when Plantinga would seem to be caught in that hopeless bind that we have just found him to be caught in--viz., that of confusing causes with reasons--it is then Wolterstorff who sallies forth with a proposal designed at once to supplement and to bolster Plantinga's account of the rationality of our human beliefs. Thus, in an essay subsequent to Plantinga's in *Faith and Rationality*, Wolterstorff seeks to introduce into the picture a notion of what he calls "belief dispositions."[32]

Now in a sense, and at first glance, this scarcely helps Plantinga's case in the least. For all that a "belief disposition" is, as Wolterstorff expounds it, is but a term to designate the sorts of causes (as contrasted with reasons) that impel us to affirm things like the existence of God, of other minds, *et al.*--and this in the absence of all reasons or evidence. Nevertheless, recognizing that the operation of such mere belief dispositions does little by way of explaining and justifying the rationality of such beliefs as are the products of these dispositions, Wolterstorff goes on to suggest that we do need to have a way of testing such dispositions, in order to determine whether they are, as he says, "reliable" or not. And, to this end, Wolterstorff apparently adapts to his own purposes a version of Alvin Goldman's epistemological theory of "reliablism." Moreover, it would seem that the tests to be used for the reliability of our beliefs amount to what in effect are little more than pragmatic tests. Thus, in the case of our belief in the existence of physical objects, say, what we would need to do would be to try to determine whether believing in such objects would on the whole "work better" or enable us, as it were, to "get around better" in the world, or "make our way better" in the world, than not believing in such objects.

And so, to use a somewhat analogous, even if rather crude, example, consider the relative payoff pragmatically of astronomers' believing that the planets move in elliptical orbits, as opposed to their believing that they move in circular orbits. For one thing, will not the mathematics of calculating the positions of the planets at different times be vastly simplified, if astronomers were to operate on the assumption of the planets moving in elliptical rather than circular orbits, with all of the complications that the latter would entail by way of having to posit epicycles upon epicycles? Very well, would it not then likewise seem that what Wolterstorff is proposing to do is to acknowledge that merely to exhibit the causes of our beliefs in terms of belief dispositions is not enough by way of insuring the rationality of such beliefs? Instead, we need also to invoke pragmatic tests to determine the reliability of such beliefs, before we can properly assess their rationality.

And yet is Wolterstorff right in this? After all, one wonders whether merely to offer ways and means and tests for determining the pragmatic reliability of our beliefs is quite the same thing as establishing the rationality of those beliefs. For, presumably, that any belief of ours should be held to be a rational belief must surely mean that we consider we have reasons for believing it to be true. And yet but a little reflection should suffice to remind us that the mere fact a belief of ours has been shown to be pragmatically reliable by no means implies that we have therefore really compelling reasons for supposing it to be true.[33]

Thus consider again our well-worn example of the issue concerning the orbits of the planets (whether they move in circular or in elliptical orbits): if the pragmatic reliability of a theory is all that counts, then it makes not the slightest difference whether in fact or in truth the planets really move in elliptical orbits or not. Rather all that matters is that on the one hypothesis our scientific calculation and manipulations would be greatly facilitated and simplified, as compared with what they would be on the other hypothesis.

And here I find it hard not to quote what has long seemed to be a singularly illuminating passage from Quine:

> As an empiricist I continue to think of the conceptual scheme of science as a tool, ultimately, for predicting future experience in the

> light of past experience. Physical objects are conceptually imported into the situation as covenient intermediaries--not by definition in terms of experience, but simply as irreducible posits comparable, epistemologically, to the gods of Homer. For my part I do, *qua* lay physicist, believe in physical objects and not in Homer's gods; and I consider it a scientific error to believe otherwise. But in point of epistemological footing the physical objects and the gods differ only in degree and not in kind. Both sorts of entities enter our conception only as cultural posits. The myth of physical objects is epistemologically superior to most in that it has proved more efficacious than other myths as a device for working a manageable structure into the flux of experience.[34]

Consider, then, the implications that a quotation such as this must have for the sort of Calvinist-Analyst epistemology that P. W. and Co. are proposing. For do P. W. and Co. really want to say that a belief in the existence of God--or likewise a belief in other minds, or in physical objects--that beliefs such as these can claim to be rationally superior beliefs in no other sense than that in which a belief in the elliptical orbits of the planets may be said to be rationally superior to a belief in the circular orbits of the planets? Yes, and still more particularly, is it P. W. and Co.'s position that all such beliefs, and particularly the belief in the existence of God, amount to no more than just so many "myths" or "cultural posits" that have established their rational superiority to other myths on no other grounds than that of their having proved to be a better "device for working a manageable structure into the flux of experience"?

Of course, it goes without saying that P. W. and Co. would doubtless draw back from any such consequence as this in both horror and dismay. And yet what alternative do they have, so long as they persist in supposing that, for our beliefs to be adjudged rational, no more is needed than that there be sufficient causes productive of those beliefs, quite irrespective of whether there be reasons for such beliefs, in the sense of reasons for supposing them to be true? Or, again, while P. and W. would doubtless say that of course a belief is not necessarily a reliable belief if there be no ground for it other than that we are psychologically disposed (i.e., have a "belief disposition") to accept it, all the same, under the conditions laid down by P. and W., what other reason would a person have for not going along with a particular belief of ours unless it be found to be not as reliable, or as pragmatically fruitful, as some alternative belief? The only trouble is that the reliability of our beliefs can be established independently of their truth. And, when the reliability of our beliefs is something thus established quite independently of their truth, the consequence can only be that such a reliability in our beliefs is hardly a substitute for the rationality of those beliefs based on considerations of their truth.

Nor would such a consequence seem to be entirely without a certain irony, so far as P. W. and Co. are concerned. For what with their tendency to rely upon merely pragmatic considerations, so far as the reliability of our belief dispositions are concerned, would not P. W. and Co. appear to have thrown themselves right into the arms of Richard Rorty and the currently fashionable pragmatism of so-called Post-Analytic philosophy?

Oh, it's true that, in the very Introduction to *Faith and Rationality*,[35] Wolterstorff remarks on how "some philosophers [notably Rorty] have concluded from the collapse of the classical foundationalist theory of knowledge that the concept of knowledge itself must be discarded." Still other philosophers (e.g., Feyerabend), Wolterstorff continues, "have concluded from the collapse of the classical foundationalist theory of rationality that the distinction between rational and non-rational beliefs must be discarded." But Wolerstorff vigorously protests that, so far as P. W. and Co. are concerned, though they of course reject Foundationalism, they nevertheless do not wish to go as far as either Rorty or Feyerabend.

But maybe P. W. and Co. have no choice! For have we not now seen that, in their rejection of Foundationalism, there is no way in which P. W. and Co. can show their basic propositions to have any proper evidence in their support; and, as for the so-called belief dispositions which they would invoke as being grounds of our beliefs, these provide only causes for our beliefs and not reasons for them at all. Hence, for P. W. and Co., there can be no justification for their beliefs other than the largely non-cognitive justification of Pragmatism and Reliablism. And what else must this betoken if not that P. W. and Co. have thereby indeed simply handed themselves over, roped and bound, into the hands of Rorty and Co., and of his Post-Analytic philosophers? *Facilis descensus Averno!*

F. Where Did P. W. and Co. Make Their Wrong Turning?

And now for what would seem to be an obvious question. Granted that P. W. and Co. would appear to have simply made a wrong turning somewhere along the line in their prolonged and laborious efforts to provide an alternative account of just what it is that makes for the rationality of our human beliefs, just where and at what point did this wrong-turning take place? Notice that this question of ours is not one as to why P. W. and Co. made the wrong turning that they did. For, on the matter of the "why," we have already seen that the reason P. W. and Co. made their decision to turn away from anything like the traditional Thomistic account of human rationality is that they were dissatisfied with the Foundationalism, and more specifically with the Foundationalist Principle, that underlies this Thomistic account. For recall that what the Foundationalist Principle underscores, so far as any account of knowledge and rationality is concerned, is that in order for any of our human beliefs--particularly our non-religious beliefs--to be fully rational, they must rest upon sufficient evidence. And this means, according to the way the Foundationalist Principle is then interpreted by P. W. and Co., that the rationality of our beliefs must needs be understood either in terms of a self-evidence, or in terms of an evidence that is derived from principles that are self-evident. But, of course, P. W. and Co. will have none of this.

All right, but, in turning away from the Foundationalist Principle, P. W. and Co. quickly found themselves being led right down the garden path to their highly incredible and seemingly indefensible theory of so-called basic propositions, these being propositions for which presumably we have neither reason nor evidence, but which notwithstanding we are said to have every reason to accept, and to be entirely rational in so accepting. Very well, then, but just how did P. W. and Co. come to make this seemingly preposterous turn to so-called "basic propositions," and just where and at what point was it that this wrong turning of theirs was made?

Well, presumably the wrong turning was made at that point where, as regards physical-object statements, or statements about other minds (or about God), it seemed that the sensory evidence which we are presented with in our experince turns out not to be a sufficient evidence, or even any evidence at all, of the existence of physical objects (or, *mutatis mutandis*, of other minds, or of God, etc.). And yet, for all of that, it was recognized that we cannot very well avoid making judgments as to the existence of physical objects (confining our attention to this particular type of example for the moment). Hence P. W. and Co. come out with their baffling pronouncement that our belief in the existence of physical objects must therefore be taken to represent one of their much vaunted "basic propositions"--these being propositions for which we have no reason or evidence of any kind (they being neither self-evident, nor empirically evident, nor evident as a result of any kind of inference), but which notwithstanding we have every reason to accept. And that, as we have already insisted, is simply fantastic!

Clearly, though, we should now be able to see that this wrong turning by P. W. and Co. was made precisely at that point where it seemed as if, to take a particular example, we were indeed presented in our sensory experience with all sorts of visual and auditory and tactual data, and yet not at all with the physical object or objects that it might be supposed sustained such data. As a result, it was said that, while of course we might be said to see the green of the leaf perfectly well, as well as its size, position, etc., the leaf itself we do not see. Nor is it even in principle possible actually to *see* such a thing as a leaf, as contrasted, say, with its color. And no more is it possible, given the circumstances of perception and perceptual experience, as P. W. and Co. understand them, that the existence of such a thing as a leaf is in any way inferable from the perceivable data of the leaf either. Accordingly, it is precisely at this juncture that P. W. and Co. make their wrong turning. For, not being able to claim either any direct perceptual evidence or any inferential evidence of any kind for the existence of the leaf, P. W. and Co. in effect declare that there is just no way under heaven--or even in heaven either presumably--for us to get from the green that we see with our eyes to the leaf that we know the green to be the color of. And so what do they do but simply go ahead and posit the existence of the leaf as a physical object anyway.

Accordingly, we suggest that it is just this bald, bare positing of the existence of the leaf that is the wrong turning that P. W. and Co. are guilty of. What's more, having thus posited that there is a leaf, P. W. and Co. then declare such a positing or affirmation to be in the nature of a "basic proposition;" and a basic proposition, they say, is one that one has every reason to accept and is entirely rational in accepting, even though, seemingly by the very same logic of their position, there is no reason of any kind for accepting it. And what is that if not a hopeless epistemological predicament from which there is for P. W. and Co. seemingly just no exit!

G. But Was Not the Wrong-Turning a Thing at Once Gratuitous and Unnecessary?

But contrast now the way in which this transition from mere perceptual data to a rational understanding of the objects of which those data are the data is both described and justified in the Thomistic tradition. And indeed, to this end, why do we not simply undertake to work with that trivial and all-too-shopworn example which we have already alluded to? This is the example of my seeing with my eyes the green of the leaf, and then coming to recognize that, as Aristotle or Aquinas would understand the situation here, the leaf is what Aristotle would call a substance, or what contemporary philosophers might simply call a physical object. Nor is it to be denied that the leaf, as a substance or as a physical object, is not as such anything that we are presented with by the so-called external senses or the common sense at least not just as such. No, that we should actually come to see a substance, such as a leaf or a tree, requires an intellectual apprehension or cognition, no less than a simultaneous sensory cognition as well.

Thus, for instance, when I look at the leaf on the tree outside my window I certainly can see with my eyes the green color. But this greenness I, in turn, am certainly able to recognize as being a color; and a color is certainly a quality. Not only that but, it being my intellectual faculties of apprehension that are now being called into play, along with my sensory faculties, does it not immediately become evident to me--yes, intellectually or rationally evident, if you will--that the green color that I am perceiving being a quality, that quality cannot as such be a quantity? No, nor is the green color just as such an action either, any more than it is a quantity, or a relation, or a place, or a time. For, after all, I surely am able to recognize intellectually that the green color I am now being presented with in my sensory perception is a quality, and that a quality is an accident and not a substance, and that an accident such as a quality is not to be confused with other accidents, such as quantities, or relations, or actions, or places, or whatever.

And then, of course, and still more importantly, just as intellectually it is nothing if not evident to me that qualities are not quantities, or quantities actions, etc., so also is it nothing if not evident that every quality must be the quality of something? And, no less than qualities, so also must any and every quantity be the quantity of something, just as any action has to be the action of some agent. Likewise, that of which the quality is a quality, or the quantity a quantity, or the action an action, can be nothing other than the sort of thing Aristotle called a substance.

And lo, what have we here if not a whole cluster of self-evident truths, as, for example, the undeniable truth that there simply could not be any such thing as a green color without its being the green of something, viz., of a substance? To be sure, the existence of the substance of which the green is the color is not made evident to me as a knower in the way in which the green is made known; instead, it is "seen," or intellectually apprehended, directly in conjunction with my sensory apprehension of the several sensory qualities that are all perceived in the leaf outside my window.

And, with this, is not our point established? Our human cognitive faculties are such that our faculties of intellectual insight quite patently function in close conjunction with our sensory faculties; as a result, we not only see the green with our eyes, but we also recognize, through an intellectual insight, that there is a physical object out there that is thus green. Accordingly, from this standpoint what could be more gratuitous than the incredible straining at gnats and swallowing of camels that P. W. and Co. would appear to have gone through, in order to explain how from sensory perceptions we are led--as it would seem quite irrationally--to an actual positing of physical objects. These latter, as P. W. and Co. describe things, we neither see with our eyes nor apprehend intellectually with our intelligence. Rather it takes nothing less than a supposed "belief disposition" to somehow impel us or cause us just to up and posit the physical object. And, of course, such a positing is nothing if not somehow all but in vain, since it provides us with not the slighest evidence for the existence of the physical object. Nor is what Quine calls the "posit" of such an object warranted by anything more than merely pragmatic considerations. In fact, the object must literally be reckoned as only a posit, and not as a fact, there being no evidence of any kind of the actual existence of anything like a real physical object or substance. At least, that is the way the situation shapes up on the account given by P. W. and Co.

Nevertheless, it is just here and at this point that the Thomist must needs, for his part, be wary of a criticism to the effect that, on the account which he and we would give of our human empirical knowledge of things or substances in the world, the Thomist has admittedly introduced directly into that account a contention to the effect that, alongside our perceptual faculties, there must also be operative an actual faculty of rational or intellectual insight. But no sooner do we Thomists make a move of this sort than immediately, it would seem, we have got ourselves caught up in an irrevocable *a priorism* reminiscent of Descartes, as a result of which any and all supposed rational or intellectual knowledge would need to be adjudged somehow innate, and thus in no wise dependent upon our perceptual experience at all. Surely, though, any such accusations of an *a priorism* and of a Cartesian certainty and indubitability with respect to all knowledge--such accusations must surely be wide of the mark when aimed at an epistemology of the Thomistic type. For is it not patent from the account which we have just given of the operation of what we have termed "intellectual insight,"[36] and which is characteristic of the Thomistic tradition, that such an insight involves no less than an actual recognition and discernment in the green color that is perceived that this same perceied green is the green of a physical object? Accordingly, the insight involved is no less than an insight into the very object of the sensory perception, and an insight that would be simply impossible without the antecedent perception that provides our intellectual insight with the very materials that it has to work on.

Nor need one suppose either that, because this intellectual insight is an operation that is truly intellectual and not merely sensory, its operation must therefore be, as it were, invariably infallible and always sure-fire. Far from it, for the green which I see--to recur to this trivial example again--and which I take to be the green of a leaf, I could well be mistaken about: it could conceivably turn out to be the green only of a piece of felt, and not of a leaf at all. Nor is that all either, for (granted that there is indeed a sense in which, in my coming to recognize intellectually that the green which I see must needs be the green of a physical object or a substance, and that the implicit truth contained therein is certainly a self-evident one), even so, and even as regards such clearly self-evident principles as those pertaining to substances and their accidents, or things and their properties, we need constantly to be on the lookout lest we misconstrue or misapply them. For, as we have already remarked, from the history of science and philosophy anyone can come up with countless examples of principles that seemed to be unquestionably evident, and thus nothing if not *per se nota,* and that nevertheless later turned out to be not so at all.

Moreover, having said this much, we can perhaps now begin to understand just how and why P. W. and Co. should have been so led astray in their supremely confident and implacable criticisms of Aristotelian and Thomistic Foundationalism. For they took such a Foundationalism, together with the Foundationalist Principle which is the core of that Foundationalism, as if it did no less than set up an absolute standard of rationality, such that if any item of our would-be human knowledge were to fail, even in any respect, to meet the standard of self-evidence (or else to be derivative from the self-evident) then that item of supposed knowledge could not qualify as a rational knowledge at all.

But this is a wholly unwarranted construction that P. W. and Co. have placed upon the Foundationalist Principle. Clearly, their interpretation reflects the unfortunate Rationalist or Cartesian way of reading the Principle, and completely overlooks the way the Principle was always regarded as functioning in a Thomistic or Aristotelian context. For never should it be lost sight of that in the view of Aristotle and Aquinas all human knowledge must proceed from our perceptual experience. As a result, there is just no way in which human knowledge could ever be reckoned as being an affair of innate ideas, or of any sort of Platonic *anamnesis,* much less an affair of mere analytic truths in the Kantian sense.

True, considered ideally, it perhaps is scarcely enough, on the Thomistic view, for example, that something should only be observed to be the case; it also needs to be understood why it is the case. Accordingly, for such a rational understanding in the fullest sense, our beliefs could well be said to need to be either self-evident in themselves, or else derivatively evident from truths that are thus self-evident. Still, that but states the goal and the ideal of a fully rational knowledge, to which generally in our human scientific and rational understandings we but aspire, and yet seldom, and in only occasional instances, attain.

And so it is that, if all truth--and such is the constant Thomistic contention--must needs arise out of experience, it is both difficult and but rarely that, in such things as are but empirically evident to us, we can detect, be it either through a direct insight, or through an induction leading to such insight, anything that is truly and unmistakably rationally evident in the sense of a self-evidence. And so it is, to revert again to our familiar but continuingly trivial example, that the green that I see with my eyes, when I examine the leaf on a tree, is indeed green. But is it the green of a leaf? As regards this, of course, I may be mistaken. True, it is perhaps self-evident that the green which I see cannot but be the green of something, i.e., of some physical object or substance; but it certainly is not self-evident that the green that I see must be the green of a leaf. Granted, in past experiences, in like situations, the kind of green which I now see has turned out to be the green of a leaf. And yet do I really know, in the sense of having a truly evident knowledge, that this time the green that I see is the green of a leaf, or even just what a leaf is? Of course not, for such a knowledge can only be built up as a result of inductions from experience, and these are ever fallible and subject to correction. Occasionally, to be sure, and usually on a level of high generality, my inductions from experience may culminate in what has sometimes been called an Aristotelian "intuitive induction,"[37] in which one recognizes that the color that one sees is a quality, and that a quality must be the quality of something, of a substance. But even self-evidence of this sort, as we have already noted, could well turn out to be unexpectedly fallible after all, it always being possible that what seems self-evident to us might turn out not really to be so.

In any case, we surely now need say no more either in rebuttal of the kind of Calvinist-Analyst epistemology that P. W. and Co. have proposed in *Faith and Rationality,* or in support of that traditional and rival Thomistic account of rationality that P. W. and Co. are so concerned to repudiate. For by this time it certainly should be apparent that the reasons for their repudiation turn out not to be really reasons at all, and their substitute concept of human rationality, which P. W. and Co. would put in place of the more traditional Thomistic account, turns out to be not so much a mistake as almost a complete disaster. And so, as Mark Twain might say, is not the most charitable thing that we might now do simply "draw the curtain" on the sorry spectacle of P. W. and Co.'s proposed Calvinist-Analyst variety of epistemology?

Professor Emeritus

Center for Thomistic Studies

NOTES

1. Kierkegaard's *Concluding Unscientific Postscript*, translated by Swenson (Princeton: Princeton University Press, 1944) 305.

2. *Faith and Rationality: Reason and belief in God*, edited by Alvin Plantinga and Nicholas Wolterstorff (Notre Dame and London: University of Notre Dame Press, 1983). Henceforth *FR*, throughout this volume.

3. Be it noted that what follows is only an exhibit of the sort of argument involved, not a defense of it. Nor is anything like a full-dress defense attempted anywhere either in this essay or in the ones that follow, this being not to our immediate purpose in this volume. Nevertheless, readers are referred to R. J. Connell, "Preliminaries to the Five Ways," in this volume, as fundamental to any right understanding of the sorts of demonstrations that are attempted in traditional natural theology.

4. *Per se notum* is used throughout this volume for the singular of what is known *per se*, and *per se nota* for its plural, regardless of the gender of the Latin word translating the English word to which the expression applies.

5. Cf. note 3 above.

6. *Faith and Rationality*, pp. 1 and 4.

7. For confirmation of how such a response is nothing but the obvious one for a Thomist to make, see H. DuLac, "A First Incredulous Reaction to *Faith and Rationality*," in this volume.

8. *FR*, 46.

9. *FR*, 138-139.

10. *FR*, 139.

11. *Summa Theologiae*, II-II, 5, 2.

12. *S.T.*, II-II, 2, 10. The translation is largely that of Anton C. Pegis in the Random House edition of *The Basic Writings of St. Thomas Aquinas.*

13. Perhaps it is somewhat gratuitous that we should bear down thus hard on P. W. and Co. for their seeming to make so much of their charge that Aquinas is, after all, no more than an Evidentialist. Indeed, there are occasional passages even in *Faith and Rationality* where first Plantinga, and then Wolterstorff, would seem to qualify at least somewhat their charge of Evidentialism as directed at St. Thomas. Nevertheless, to recognize that on this point there may well have been, not just a certain qualification of this charge on the part at least of Wolterstorff, but perhaps even an almost complete change of heart and mind, one might do well to consult a volume later than *Faith and Rationality*, entitled *Rationality, Religious Belief, and Moral Commitment,* edited by Andi and Wainwright, published in 1986 by Cornell University Press. In it Wolterstorff would seem quite to withdraw his earlier charges of Evidentialism, as these were aimed at Aquinas. But, even more significant, in the same volume there is an essay by Kenneth Konyndyk, a staunch Calvinist, to be sure, and a colleague of Wolterstorff at Calvin College, in which he, Konyndyk, carefully examines the evidence against Aquinas that he might have been an Evidentialist; and Konyndyk comes out declaring emphatically that Aquinas was presumably just not an Evidentialist at all. Still more decisive, however, is the testimony of still another Calvinist, Arvin Vos, in a volume published in 1985 by the University of Notre Dame Press, entitled *Aquinas, Calvin, and Contemporary Protestant Thought.* This balanced and well-researched volume does nothing if not drive the last nail in the coffin of P. W. and Co.'s utterly wrong-headed notion that St. Thomas might possibly be interpreted as having been little more than an Evidentialist.

14. See especially T. D. Sullivan, "Adequate Evidence for Religious Assent," in this volume.

15. Plantinga's charge that Foundationalism as understood by St. Thomas turns out to be self-referentially inconsistent is developed principally in Section D of Part II of "Reason and Belief in God." See *FR*, 59-63.

16. *FR*, 46.

17. For a rather different assessment of Plantinga's charge of self-referential inconsistency as leveled against what is presumed to be Thomistic Foundationalism, see J. Boyle, "Is 'God Exists' a Properly Basic Belief?", in this volume.

18. The examples which follow are among those Plantinga gives of self-evident truths. See *FR*, 55-56.

19. *FR*, 56.

20. It might be mentioned just in passing that some years ago I undertook a direct critique of the widespread notion that any truth that may be adjudged to be self-evident must for that reason be in the nature of what Kant called "analytic truths," and therefore could not possibly be in any way informative, or a truth about the world. See my *Two Logics* (Evanston: Northwestern University Press, 1969) 71 ff.

21. See Immanuel Kant, *Critique of Pure Reason*, trans. Norman Kemp Smith (London: Macmillan, 1929), Introduction, Sect. IV, B 11.

22. On this, see Plantinga, *FR*, 87-91.

23. On the analogy between belief in God as simply a basic proposition and belief in physical objects, or in other minds, as being likewise propositions which are to be reckoned as basic, see Plantinga, *FR*, 75-82.

24. For a rather different treatment and assessment of Plantinga's reliance on basic propositions, see J. Boyle, "Is 'God Exists' a Properly Basic Belief?", in this volume.

25. It needs to be remarked that, while Plantinga insists that we can have no reasons for our belief in God (or in physical objects, or in other minds), we may not for that reason say that such beliefs of ours are therefore "groundless." See Plantinga, *FR*, 82, for example. As we shall see presently, this seemingly rather paradoxical assertion of Plantinga's that, while we are without reasons for believing in God, we are not without grounds for such a belief--this is all to be explained by the fact that, although we have no reason for believing that God exists, we are nevertheless impelled to believe this by certain causal forces operating upon us.

26. It is not without significance that, in his essay in *Faith and Rationality* entitled *"Jerusalem and Athens Revisited," George Mavrodes* does chide Plantinga and Wolterstorff with just such a confusion of causes with reasons. However, Mavrodes seems not to press this point home--at least not in this particular essay.

27. Quoted in *FR*, 65-66.

28. *FR*, 66.

29. *FR*, 90, stress added.

30. *FR*, 90.

31. *New Essays in Philosophical Theology*, edited by Flew and MacIntyre (New York: The MacMillan Company, 1955) 99-100.

32. See "Can Belief in God Be Rational?", *FR*, esp. 139-169.

33. This is not to imply that in pragmatism there is no theory of truth. Rather the point is that "truth" for a pragmatist does not have the same sense as it has, say, for a traditional defender of something like a so-called correspondence theory of truth.

34. Willard Van Orman Quine, *From a Logical Point of View: Logico-Philosophical Essays* (Cambridge, Mass.: Harvard University Press) 44.

35. *Ibid.*, 4-5.

36. For a further and more sophisticated discussion of this notion of "intellectual insight" and how it operates, the reader is referred to T. Russman, "'Reformed' Epistemology," in this volume.

37. Of course, this is not a term that Aristotle ever uses, and yet what the term signifies is brought out effectively in the famous concluding chapter (Chapter 19) of Book II of the *Posterior Analytics*.

AN INCREDULOUS FIRST REACTION TO *FAITH AND RATIONALITY*

Henri Dulac

It seems to me that any discussion about the relation of human reason, or "rationality," to the acceptance of knowledge about God has to take into account three distinct problems: (1) whether "God exists" can be known by the human intellect unaided by revelation; (2) whether "God exists" and other propositions about God that can be known by the human intellect unaided by revelation can also be known by faith, i.e., by God's word; (3) whether propositions such as "God is triune" or "Christ is the Redeemer of mankind" can be known by the human intellect unaided by faith. In my reading of *Faith and Rationality* I do not find these issues consistently distinguished from one another. At times I do find some recognition of the need for making some distinctions, but I do not find the distinctions consistently made.

Certainly St. Thomas Aquinas was extremely careful to keep these issues distinct from each other. This is evident both from his explicitly philosophical writings (mostly commentaries on works of Aristotle) and from his theological writings in which he sometimes recounts philosophical arguments for propositions which can also be known by divine revelation.

Although the book contains frequent references to St. Thomas Aquinas and seems somewhat preoccupied with positions taken by him, I find the attempts to present those positions inadequate, and I shall try to draw attention to some of these points.

At least one matter of terminology needs to be clarified before one can approach any of these issues--at least if one's approach includes reference to St. Thomas's writings. Since the time of John Locke the word "belief" has been used to refer to any proposition accepted by a holder of the belief, regardless of the justification for it. In this sense I can say "I believe what I just wrote in the last sentence to be true." St. Thomas, on the other hand, uses "belief" (*fides*) or the verb *credo* and its cognates, e.g., *credibile*, in a much more restricted way in speaking about a proposition accepted on the word of another person, human or divine. For St. Thomas such a proposition is accepted not because of evidence of the object, but because of some evidence extrinsic to the object; he is careful to distinguish *fides* from *scientia*. A proposition accepted on the basis of extrinsic evidence that renders a human proponent credible can never be more than probable, and St. Thomas would regard such a proposition in the same way as he would regard other probable propositions.

For St. Thomas an effort to establish the existence of God by argument is a part of what Aristotle called First Philosophy, which later came to be known as Metaphysics. The conclusion of such an argument does not pretend to arrive at a belief in his sense of the word, but at what he would call scientific knowledge, i.e., certain knowledge based on evidence. Such an argument must be judged purely philosophically and not as it might lead to an act of faith.

Mr. Plantinga seems to regard "self-evident" propositions as simply "easily known." It would be quite inaccurate to regard that as St. Thomas's view. St. Thomas is clear that a proposition *per se notum* is one in which the predicate is contained in the definition of the subject. If one takes the propositions (13) to (23) that Plantinga has on pages 55 and 56, it seems to me that St. Thomas would recognize only 19 (The whole is greater than the part) and 20 (Man is an animal) as *per se nota*. Proposition 14 (No man is both married and unmarried) could be regarded as the principle of non-contradiction stated in a restricted subject matter. The fact that Plantinga regards "Man is an animal" as dubiously self-evident I think shows that he has a notion of self-evident at variance from what St. Thomas regards as *per se notum*. For St. Thomas, *per se nota* propositions may not be easy to know at all; Plantinga recognizes that St. Thomas indicates that some propositions are *per se nota quoad sapientes* and others *quoad omnes*. Since the *per se notum* status of a proposition depends on the predicate's being part of the definition of the subject, the lack of a precise knowledge of the definition of the subject would prevent a knower from knowing the proposition as *per se notum*. A precise knowledge of the definition of "man" might indeed be hard to come by and in any case would require an exhaustive search in order to guarantee its accuracy. St. Thomas is not setting out criteria for ease of knowing propositions, but rather criteria for scientific knowledge. He is simply doing what Aristotle did in the *Posterior Analytics*, chap. 2 (St. Thomas's commentary, Lect. 4-6) and chap. 4 (commentary, Lect. 9-11). Such knowledge of a subject is necessary if one is going to prove that a property belongs to a subject, e.g., that the property "having interior angles equal two right angles" belongs to "triangle." This kind of proof or demonstration he calls "demonstration by proper cause" or "*propter quid*." The argument or arguments for the existence of God are not of this type. They are rather arguments from effect to cause, i.e., they attempt to arrive at knowledge of the existence of a cause on which some observable effect depends. They do not demonstrate a property of a subject whose definition is previously known.

The first of the other two issues is whether "God exists" and other propositions about God that can be known by the human intellect unaided by faith can also be known by faith, i.e., by God's word. In the *Summa Contra Gentiles*, Book I, chap. 4, as well as in other places, St. Thomas points out that it was fitting for God to propose even these truths that can be naturally known. Why? Because most people are too dull, too busy, or too lazy to discover them by the use of their own intellects, and these natural truths are too important to permit such wide-spread ignorance. Natural theology is not everyone's cup of tea, and even those who attempt to brew it often have a pretty thin beverage.

Mr. Wolterstorff has things backward when he alleges:

> But the goal of natural theology for Aquinas was exactly the same as for Anselm: to transmute what one already believed into something known. . . . They were engaged in the transmutation project of altering belief (faith) into knowledge (p. 141).

I cannot speak of what St. Anselm precisely had in mind, but I think St. Thomas makes it clear that arguments made by unaided human reason can be given for certain propositions that God has also chosen to reveal. One intellect cannot have evident knowledge and not have evident knowledge of the same truth at one and the same time, and therefore does not have an act of science and an act of faith about the same object at the same time. However, that problem would arise for very few people, since very few people would actually have evident (demonstrated) knowledge of the truths of natural theology. If, by hypothesis, someone, e.g., presumably St. Thomas himself, did have demonstrated knowledge about a truth of natural theology, he would assent to it by reason of the evidence he had in his metaphysical reasoning. I shall comment later on the influence his divine faith might have on his assent.

I found Plantinga's quotations from the nineteenth century Dutch theologian, Herman Bavinck, on the whole an excellent presentation of what I judge to be the correct view of the relation between natural theology and divine revelation. I think it is also the view of St. Thomas. Plantinga twice quotes Bavinck: "Scripture . . . does not make God the conclusion of a syllogism, leaving it to us whether we think the argument holds or not. But it speaks with authority. Both theologically and religiously it proceeds from God as the starting point" (pp. 64 and 71). St. Thomas would certainly agree with the Reformed thinkers that the "rightness of belief in God in no way depends upon the success or availability of the sort of theistic arguments that form the natural theologian's stock in trade" (p. 72).

Bavinck, as well as Karl Barth, recognizes the utter transcendence of supernatural truth. By supernatural truth I mean truths about the Trinity, the Incarnation, Christ's redemption of man, the grace which Christ won for us and which He grants us to transform us, and our supernatural destiny of eternal happiness with Him. On this issue, no one has been more emphatic about the completely supernatural character of such knowledge than St. Thomas. The human intellect is in no way capable of reaching such knowledge by the exercise of human rationality. For such knowledge (I use the word generically, not to designate science; the Latin word would be *cognitio*) we are dependent on the word of God; our act of assenting to such propositions is an act of faith (*Summa Theologiae*, II-II, q. 2, a. 3). The word of God alone is the motive for assent to such truths. Such assent is not dependent on a prior knowledge of natural theology.

There were perhaps some theologians in the past who thought of the ultimate assent of divine faith as a kind of smooth progress from natural theology through apologetic arguments for Christianity to the final assent of divine faith, but St. Thomas was clearly not one of them. Such a view proceeds as if the posterior step were always dependent upon the prior, and as if one were dealing with a homogeneous kind of rational procedure, with a homogeneous kind of evidence at each stage, resulting in a homogeneous series of conclusions. It seems to me that Bavinck, Barth, and Calvin himself find this conception just as unacceptable as St. Thomas does.

However, the alternative is not to deny the problem by slipping off into some new kinds of "basic propositions." It is a little hard to know just what Plantinga thinks are the attributes of a "basic proposition" when he suggests that "I had breakfast more than an hour ago" is such a proposition. If my own very fallible memory or that of my absent-minded colleagues is to be taken as producing "basic propositions," I am afraid "belief in God" is in worse shape than it has ever been in. Would it not seem ludicrous or worse to the garden variety of academic today or any other day? Particularly since the objector would merely be content to say, "I just don't see that it is universally accepted."

Rather than deny that human reason has anything whatever to do with making an act of faith, perhaps it would be more productive to examine other acts of faith we make which have nothing to do with divine faith. Let us say I encounter an unusually pleasant Hoosier whose judgment I come to respect (partly, I must admit, because it often coincides with mine). He tells me that southern Indiana is a lovely country of rolling hills, green forests, quaint bridges, and streams and lakes crowded with bass. Now, my own experience is limited to the northern part of the state--an area hardly known for the most enticing terrain in North America. With regard to evidence about southern Indiana my intellect is at best agnostic--with perhaps even a little inclination to disbelieve in is attractiveness. However, my congenial Hoosier has in the past been reliable in his judgments: he recommended a good restaurant in Washington, he suggested a good lecturer for my college, he likes Jane Austen. I am inclined to regard his judgment as sound. It appears to me to be "a good thing" to accept his judgment and to assent to the proposition, "Southern Indiana is charming." What I have done is to make an assent without evidence of the object but with evidence that is outside the object--namely, the reliability of the speaker. Thus, "Southern Indiana is charming" becomes credible to me, because I have experience of the speaker's making good judgments at other times, and I now find it good for me to accept his judgment on this point. I make an act of human faith in the charm of southern Indiana; the motive for my assent is the word of my congenial friend. Am I certain of the charm of the area? Emphatically not. My friend is fallible. I too am fallible in judging the evidence of his past judgments. Is my acceptance of the charm of southern Indiana sufficient for me to make a detour to see for myself the next time I am driving south? Yes, I would regard it as a prudent decision to treat myself to the charms of the area even at the risk of possibly being disappointed. That is the sort of assent we make by human faith--an act of belief.

I might make somewhat the same judgment about the area by consulting a map and noting that it is near the Ohio River, and recalling that the terrain on either side of a river is frequently picturesque. Such a judgment would be no more certain than the judgment based on my friend's word. Both would be at best probable. In neither case would I have evidence of the object but in each case something outside the actual object would incline me to assent to the proposition, "Southern Indiana is charming."

I think it is something like this that better explains what John Calvin has in mind than an appeal to instinct. A child growing up in a household where God is taken seriously accepts God's presence and influence readily because of his reliance on his parents' word. Similarly, an adult marvels at the skies and readily regards the cause of such wonders as something transcending his experience. The first is an act of faith and, insofar as it depends on the parents' word, it is an act of human faith. The second is an act of probable reasoning, simple and informal though it be; but there is no necessary and evident connection made between the evidence perceived and the conclusion.

When one reads or hears the word of God, many factors can impress us to establish its credibility. I shall not review the various elements that have formed the apologist's "stock in trade" over the centuries. I suppose most often the hearer is impressed by the evident goodness of the one presenting the word of God. In recent years Malcolm Muggeridge has indicated that Mother Theresa has had this effect on him. But, whatever the hearer or viewer perceives, it seems good to him to accept the propositions being presented. Now, in making the assent of divine faith, the motive for the assent is the word of God; the human proposer is merely the instrument, albeit an important one. The crucial thing, however, is that the intellect is moved to assent not because of evidence of the object but because of something outside the object. Assent is judged to be "a good thing." The will is inclined toward that good and moves the intellect to make its assent. The reasonableness of that move is found in the judgment of credibility preceding the will's moving the intellect to assent. Notice that this is "rationality," not in the sense that something is proven but more in the sense that it is prudent to embrace this good.

In the case of making the assent of divine faith, the "good thing" that attracts the prospective believer is the possibility of eternal happiness which God has promised to believers. It is worth noting that this good is the same as the good of theological hope; it is the good which is the believer's own happiness rather than the good of theological charity, which is God Himself, an object to which all possessors of grace can be united (*I Cor.* 13:13; *Heb. 11:1; Summa Theologiae*, II-II, q. 4, a. 1c; a. 7c and ad 5).

Since supernatural happiness transcends merely human capability to achieve, and since knowledge of the possibility of that happiness transcends the power of the unaided human intellect, Catholic doctrine (and certainly St. Thomas's theology) insists that the impetus moving the will to bring the intellect to make the assent of divine faith has to be the grace of God--i.e., something supernatural and dependent on the will of God. However, that is another issue.

What I have said about the assent of divine faith applies whether one is dealing with a proposition which can be known only by divine revelation or with a proposition which can also be known by human reasoning. In neither case is the assent of divine faith dependent on reasoning about the object known. As I said earlier, one intellect cannot both be moved by evidence and not be moved by evidence of the same object at the same time. If the natural theologian assents to a proposition by the evidence presented to his intellect, and the same person also is prepared to assent to whatever is revealed by God's word, that person does not lose the merit of the act of divine faith, even though he assents because of evidence of the object (*Summa Theologiae*, II-II, q. 2, a. 10).

College of St. Thomas

St. Paul, Minnesota

ADEQUATE EVIDENCE FOR RELIGIOUS ASSENT

Thomas D. Sullivan

I. Introduction

The occasion of this volume of essays recalls the problem to which John Henry Newman drew attention in his *Grammar of Assent*. If, as John Locke and others had taught, it is not only illogical but immoral to "entertain any proposition with greater assurance than the proofs it is built on will warrant," then in honesty no one can give unqualified assent to natural or revealed religious truth. Though the Christian Locke had no desire to attack religious belief as such, but only irrational "enthusiasm," Locke's principles furnished opponents of both natural and revealed religion a very troubling argument against wholehearted assent to any religious teaching. "The authors to whom I refer," wrote Newman, "wish to maintain that there are degrees of assent, and that, as the reasons for a proposition are strong or weak, so is the assent. It follows from this that absolute assent has no legitimate exercise, except as ratifying acts of intuition or demontrations." Assent in concrete matters should never be "without some alloy of doubt, because inference in the concrete never reaches more than probability." Indemonstrable religious belief thus must be accepted only conditionally. Unqualified adhesion is morally unjustifiable.[1]

Newman was confronting what might be termed the *a priori* argument against religious belief. The argument drives home its accusation of immorality without troubling to examine in detail the evidence for any particular religious belief. No religion can conclusively demonstrate its claims. Since respect for the truth requires that belief be proportioned to the evidence, unqualified religious assent violates a duty to truth, and is thus immoral.

Not all forms of religious belief and commitment are ruled out by the *a priori* argument. One may accept the *possibility* that a religious claim is true, or tentatively believe it is so, or act as if it were. It is only "surplusage of assurance," in Locke's terms, that is always wrong. But a surplusage of assurance is just what many religious persons show. They recite creeds that begin not with "I believe the existence of God has some probability" but "I believe in God." And their prayer is not, "Oh God, if there is a God, save my soul, if I have a soul," but, "Help me, Yahweh my God, save me since you love me."

Newman's problem, then, was this: absent a completely compelling case for any revealed religion, Christianity included, how can unconditional assent be justified without thereby justifying credulity, superstition, and bigotry?

In his *Grammar* and other public writings,[2] Newman proposed several answers to this question. I do not wish at this time to follow him through any of his better known accounts, which in many ways anticipate recent work on the foundations of religious belief. Instead I simply wish to draw attention to a striking argument Newman put forward in private correspondence, an argument which affords, I think, the only solution that at once justifies certainty with respect to indemonstrable religious doctrine while acknowledging the kernel of truth in the requirement that belief is proportioned to evidence.

The advantages of Newman's line of reasoning will perhaps best be seen against the backdrop of the claim by Alvin Plantinga, Nicholas Wolterstorff, and others[3] that religious belief may be perfectly rational and proper without any evidence at all. The order, therefore, will be as follows. First we will consider the problem a little more fully, emphasizing one important feature of religious assent frequently neglected in recent discussions. Next we will consider some of the contributions of Plantinga and Wolterstorff. Then we will take up Newman's distinctive solution to the problem.

II. The Problem of Unqualified Assent

For convenience, let us set out the *a priori argument* as follows:

(1) Unqualified religious assent is disproportionate to the evidence.

(2) It is always wrong not to proportion one's assent to the total evidence (the Proportionality Principle).

And thus:

(3) Unqualified religious assent is always wrong.

It will be noted by those familiar with recent discussions of the rationality of religious belief that this argument differs from others in its emphasis on the strength of belief.[4] In this section we will begin with this point and then consider the reasoning behind the premises.

A. The Target of the Argument: Unconditional Assent

Locke's target clearly was firm belief, and this is the way Newman understood the issue when he cited Locke's condemnation of entertaining any proposition with greater assurance than the proofs it is built on will warrant.[5] Focusing on the problem posed by strong belief preserves historical continuity. But there is a far more important reason for maintaining this focus. We want to consider the most plausible *a priori* argument against religious belief, and that requires taking more than mere belief to be the target. *A priori* arguments against weak religious belief are highly implausible.

For, if even tentative acceptance of a nonevident religious proposition is "immoral," simply because it is nonevident, then just about all our beliefs stand condemned--the hunch that the Yankees will win the pennant, the opinion that Europe has not sunk into the sea, as well as the notion that the woman who calls herself your mother is indeed your mother. On the principle that where there is no compelling evidence there is to be no assent, it will be immoral to accept even tentatively the principle itself. For the claim that nothing is to be believed at all unless it is evident or demonstrable from what is evident, seems itself to be neither. Like the unverifiable verifiability principle, such an overly severe principle would suffer self-referential incoherence.

If, on the other hand, the principle should be relaxed to allow tentative acceptance of a proposition when the evidence crosses a reasonable threshold of probability--no assent unless the evidence on balance reaches probability N--then it cannot *a priori* be claimed that the evidence for a given religious belief fails to meet the standard. One would have to investigate the actual evidence for and against the belief before condemning it. The *a priori* argument would then be functionless.[6]

Thus, a principle with a threshold set so high that extremely well grounded beliefs count as "immoral" has little or nothing to recommend it, while a principle with a more reasonably set threshold cannot rule out religious belief *a priori*. So there seems to be little to an *a priori* argument unless more than weak acceptance of a proposition is at issue.

Let us assume, then, that at issue is not the half-belief that we call a hunch or conjecture, not the sort of belief a person would be willing to give up at the first sight of a new objection or to switch sides on every half-hour as his mind rocked gently back and forth with the flow of argument. Let us assume that we are talking about absolute conviction, Newman's "unqualified adhesion," i.e., conviction that excludes all doubts.[7]

B. The First Premise

We have as much as allowed the truth of the first premise of the *a priori argument*: religious assent is disproportioned to the evidence. It may be felt that in allowing this we allow too much, slighting the evidence for religious beliefs. What about natural theology? What about miracles? Is such evidence just to be dismissed out hand?

No, but pointing to these forms of evidential support leaves the first premise of the *a priori argument* untouched. As even Aquinas observed, only a tiny minority of believers with the desire, talent, and opportunity to solve all the knotty problems of natural theology can come to know the existence and attributes of God through natural theology. This means that at most only a very small fraction of the human race believes even the primary religious truths on compelling evidence. But even these are no better off than their less philosophically-minded brothers and sisters when it comes to revealed truths altogether surpassing the power of reason to understand and demonstrate. Evidence exists for the credibility of the revelation, but not irresistible evidence. It is not strict demonstration that secures the claims of apostle, gospel, or church to speak as the oracle of God. This is why we speak of *faith*. It is will, not knowledge, that steels religious belief. As Aquinas expresses it, "faith is said to be less than scientific knowledge because faith, unlike science, lacks vision of the fact, though it has the same firmness."[8] And similarly Calvin says: "Knowledge of faith consists in assurance rather than comprehension."[9] The first premise of the *a priori argument* is true. Unqualified religious assent is disproportionate to the evidence.

C. The Second Premise

What then about the second premise--the Proportionality Precept? What can be said on its behalf?

According to some writers on the subject, little or nothing. George Mavrodes, for example, while allowing that there may well be some version of a "threshold principle" properly requiring us to believe only on evidence affording a certain level of probability, nonetheless holds that, once the threshold is attained, the strength of the belief is immaterial.

> I believe, say, two propositions, p and q. And suppose too that, while p has a probability of 0.7 and q a probability of 0.8, I believe p somewhat more strongly than I believe q. Now, it may have been unwise of me to believe p when its probability is so low as 0.7. Maybe I shouldn't even have believed q at 0.8. Or maybe it is OK to believe one or both of these. But, however that may be, what additional wrong do I do by believing p more strongly than q?
>
> Or how would I be better off if I believed more strongly? It seems hard to think of what that wrong might be, or of how that *strength* of belief, as distinct from the *fact* of belief, could be a defect in my cognitive life. In absence of a reason for thinking that there is a wrong involved here, I now suspect that there is not. That is, I suspect that we have no intellectual duty to proportion our beliefs to the evidence, and that it is not, in general, better for us to aim at such proportionality.[10]

But is it really so difficult to think up reasons for proportioning assent to the total evidence? Why not just say what comes to everyone's mind when they see someone utterly convinced of something on inconclusive evidence--that excessive confidence may well blind him to the truth? Just as there may be no necessary connection between envy and hatred, so there may be no *necessary* connection between surplusage of belief and wooden-headed rejection of contrary signs. But the first tends to lead to the second. It has been said of Philip II of Spain that no experience of the failure of his policy could shake his belief in its essential excellence. One would surmise from the chronicle of folly that fills historical volumes that there may indeed be something to the idea of proportioning belief to evidence. Surely we cannot simply reject the Proportionality Principle as if it contained no more wisdom than a precept to proportion belief to the length of your nose.

Or can we?

III. Rational Belief Without Evidence

A. The Rejection of A Challenge

In *Faith and Rationality*, Alvin Plantinga, Nicholas Wolterstorff, and others have argued that "it is entirely right, rational, reasonable, and proper to believe religious truths without any evidence or argument at all."[11] The focus of these philosophers is theism, but their thesis plainly extends to other revealed truths. Speaking of what he terms the "evidentialist challenge" to religious belief, Wolterstorff says:

> The objection can be seen as presupposing a challenge, call it the *evidentialist challenge*, to theism. And this challenge can be thought of as consisting of two claims: first, if it is not rational to accept some proposition about God then one ought not accept it; and second, it is not rational to accept propositions about God unless one does so on the basis of others of one's beliefs which provide adequate evidence for them, and with a firmness not exceeding that warranted by the strength of the evidence.[12]

The pivotal point in what I have called the *a priori argument* and what Wolerstorff calls the evidentialist challenge--Locke's Proportionality Precept--is wrong. As Wolerstorff sees it, "in these essays the evidentialist challenge of the Enlightenment is challenged and overcome."[13]

To achieve this victory Plantinga and Wolterstorff (hereafter P-W) attack what they take to be a certain mischievous conception of rational belief Plantinga calls "classical foundationalism," and Wolterstorff "modern foundationalism."[14]

Essential to foundationalism of any stripe is the notion that in any individual's noetic structure some beliefs are more fundamental than others, i.e., some are accepted on the basis of others, which in turn may be accepted on the basis of yet others, ultimately bottoming in ungrounded belief held immediately. In a rational noetic structure, basic beliefs supply adequate and proportionate evidence for nonbasic beliefs.

In the form undergirding the challenge to religious belief, properly basic beliefs meet certain narrow criteria. "A proposition p is properly basic for a person S if and only if p is either self-evident to S or incorrigible for S or evident to the senses for S."[15] Such restrictions do not rule out beliefs such as "2+1=3," "I feel dizzy," and "I seem to see a tree." But they do exclude beliefs such as that God loves us and died for us. This means that a rational religious believer must be able to generate an argument from the foundations adequate to the strength of the belief. On this account of the matter, however, few if any believers would hold their beliefs rationally.

But why, Plantinga and Wolterstorff ask, cannot belief in religious truths be lodged in the very foundations of one's noetic structure? True, belief in God does not meet the classical foundationalist's criteria for proper basicality, but why should anyone accept those criteria in the first place? After all, any number of properly foundational beliefs fail to meet those criteria. The belief that the world was not created just five minutes ago with all the evidence of its antiquity is neither self-evident nor incorrigible, nor can it be secured by irresistible argument from evidence. The same is true of belief in other minds, and the existence of substances behind appearances.[16] These things though are properly believed without evidence or argument. Why not then religious truths as well?

After all, how is it that we arrive at criteria of basicality anyway? Not *a priori*. We have to begin with paradigm cases.

> Accordingly, criteria for proper basicality must be reached from below rather than above; they should not be presented *ex cathedra* but argued to and tested by a relevant set of examples. But there is no reason to assume, in advance, that everyone will agree on the examples. The Christian will of course suppose that belief in God is entirely proper and rational; if he does not accept this belief on the basis of other propositions, he will conclude that it is basic for him and quite properly so. Followers of Bertrand Russell and Madelyn Murray O'Hare may disagree; but how is that relevant? Must my criteria, or those of the Christian community, conform to their examples? Surely not. The Christian community is responsible to *its* set of examples, not to theirs.[17]

Thus, it is a paradigm of rationality to believe without any evidence at all.

B. Two Observations on This Defense

This defense has dismayed some believers perhaps as much as it has agnostics and atheists. To refuse to limit foundational beliefs to what is evident, and to insist that the nonevident propositions such as that God loves us be properly taken as basic, seems to preserve the propriety of religious belief only by cutting the ground out from objective reasoning. Why not count anything one happens to believe in as properly foundational? Why not believe in The Great Pumpkin?

P-W have answers--well-developed answers too long to pursue in detail here. For our purposes here, we need to observe only two points.

First, there is a great danger of believers from different traditions badly misunderstanding each other. There is more that unites than divides; and language gets in the way. Neither Aquinas nor Newman, for example, are foundationalists in P-W's sense of the term.[18] Both also allow that religious belief may be properly foundational, in P-W's sense of that expression. Consider, for example, this anticipation of P-W, Newman's *Grammar of Assent*.

> Life is not long enough for a religion of inferences; we shall never have done beginning, if we determine to begin with proof. We shall ever be laying our foundations; we shall turn theology into evidences and divines into textuaries. We shall never get at our first principles. Resolve to believe nothing, and you must first prove your proofs and analyze your elements, sinking farther and farther, and finding "in the lowest depth a lower deep," till you come to the broad bosom of scepticism. I would rather be bound to defend the reasonableness of assuming that Christianity is true, than to demonstrate a moral governance for the physical world.[19]

To a large extent the *Grammar* is devoted to defending that very claim, making much of the legitimacy of acting in accord with what Wolterstoff calls our "belief dispositions."[20] Wolterstorff tells us, "A person is rationally justified in believing a certain proposition which he does believe unless he has adequate reason to cease from believing it. Our beliefs . . . are innocent until proven guilty."[21] In much the same vein Newman would say, "Of the two, I would rather have to maintain that we ought to begin with believing everything that is offered to our acceptance, than that it is our duty to doubt of everything. The former," Newman continues, "indeed seems the true way of learning. In that case, we soon discover and discard what is contradictory to itself . . . . We may expect, that when there is an honest purpose and fair talents, we shall somehow make our way forward, the error falling off from the mind, and the truth developing and occupying it."[22]

Parallels abound.[23] I suspect that, once differences are reduced by sympathetic attention to the definition of key terms, the position of Plantinga and Wolterstoff would not prove to be quite so extraordinary as it would at first appear.

But, if there is not much that the believer should object to in the P-W defense of belief without evidence, there remains a second concern: is the solution adequate? Does the no-evidence-necessary defense solve the original problem? I must admit I don't know how it could. The trouble is that little or nothing seems to follow about the propriety of deep religious conviction even if belief is properly foundational in their sense of the term.

For let us assume with P-W that it is entirely proper in some circumstances to take Christianity for granted without evidence, particularly in youth. But what the mature religious believer needs is not a defense of innocent youthful religious assent, but an answer to the question, "Should I, knowing what I now know about the teachings of Christianity and yet alive to its difficulties, firmly assent to its doctrines?" What, in other words, is one to do when counter-argument comes rolling in to awaken one philosophically? Waive it with the justification that evidence and argument properly have nothing to do with religious belief? This is not the tack taken in the end by P-W, despite all they have to say about the propriety of believing without evidence.[24] *Something* has to ground belief. And so, Plantinga writes, "my claim is that belief in God is properly basic; it does not follow, however, that it is *groundless*." Rational belief does require grounds. "Grounds" are conditions or circumstances that confer justification. The difference between "evidence" and "grounds" comes out in an example:

> If I see someone displaying typical pain behavior, I take it that he or she is in pain. Again, I do not take the displayed behavior as

> *evidence* for that belief; I do not infer that belief from others I hold; I do not accept it on the basis of other beliefs. Still, my perceiving the pain behavior plays a unique role in the formation and justification of that belief; as in the previous case [one of believing he sees a tree] it forms the ground of my justification for the belief in question.[25]

It would appear that "grounds" differ from "evidence" on Plantinga's account by reason of the fact that "evidence" is to be understood as a form of *belief*, i.e., propositionally packaged material, while grounds are not.[26] The reason a memory or sight of something doesn't count as evidence is that these experiences are not *beliefs* from which something else is inferred.

So we do not need "evidence;" instead we need "grounds." But what are "grounds"? Just triggering devices or events, as Wolterstorff seems to allow?[27] Then Smith's getting drunk would be grounds justifying his basic belief that he had a wonderful singing voice.[28] Unless "grounds" are *cognitive* grounds, i.e., unless "grounds" supply reason with information, having "grounds" says nothing for the rationality of one's beliefs. If, however, "grounds" are cognitively grasped data, they would seem to be the very stuff most people call "evidence." In that case it is hard to see how anything has been accomplished. Whether we speak of "grounds" or "evidence," the basic problem is still with us. To the no-evidence-necessary defense of Plantinga and Wolterstorff, the objector can concede that children and other innocents may accept much that is taught them without weighing the evidence, but argue that matters are much different for the mature believer. Publicly available data get expressed propositionally and offered against whatever it is that first led one to believe various propositions. Confronted with evidence and arguments against the original sources of his belief, his "grounds," the mature believer has to make a decision. Evidence and argument properly play a role in that decision. They cannot be ignored.

In the end, Plantinga acknowledges this, noting that many people are brought up to believe in God, but then encounter arguments by skeptics that threaten to defeat their belief. "If the believer is to remain justified," Plantinga tells us, "something further is called for--something that *prima facie* defeats the defeaters."[29] But what happens if the believer cannot defeat the defeater, cannot spot the fallacy in the defeater's argument, or find a reliable authority to do it for him? Perhaps, Plantinga allows, one is no longer justified in accepting theistic belief.[30] Evidence and argument trump grounds.

But what are we to do when it appears that our grounds might get trumped? Once I believed in Santa Claus. Now I do not. Presumably there was a time when I properly wavered. Is religious belief the same? Should I hold my Christian beliefs tentatively if I cannot defeat all the defeaters? Presumably not. Calvin certainly would not approve of the Christian's opening himself to doubt. The whole point of believing-without-resting-belief-on-argument is to insure that faith will not be "unstable and wavering."[31] And yet, though everything Plantinga and Wolterstorff say reflects their loyalty to this ideal of unwavering faith, it is not at all clear that in the end we have been given any reason to think that a mature person's belief should be firm.

For, oddly enough, the original question of firmness--Wolterstorff defines "evidentialism" with reference to it--appears to drop out of sight[32] as the focus shifts to the issue of proper basicality. We are told that religious belief may be properly basic, but being basic does not entail being firm. As Plantinga himself notes, "it does not follow, of course, that *p* is certain, incorrigible, unrevisable, maximally warranted, or believed more firmly than any belief that is not basic for me."[33] But if a basic belief is not necessarily firmer than any nonbasic belief, and plenty of nonbasic beliefs are not firm at all, it follows that a belief can be basic without being firm. Moreover, we have been given no reason not to waver when facing possible defeaters. Grant, then, that religious beliefs may be properly foundational in P-W's sense of the term, and you grant nothing of importance for the problem at hand. The anti-evidentialist approach was supposed to show why it is wrong to insist that the strength of one's belief should always be proportional to the strength of the evidence for that belief but, far from "overcoming" the challenge, it seems to leave the main problem entirely untouched.

Well, perhaps not quite. Though the no-evidence-necessary defense leaves us without any reason to think that under the pressure of objections the proper attitude is to hold beliefs very tentatively, perhaps Wolterstorff's defense of "credulity dispositions" does. Following Thomas Reid, Wolterstorff holds that we ought to remain committed to all our originally and innocently acquired beliefs until the situation is hopeless. We are rationally justified in believing a certain proposition which we believe unless we have adequate reason for refraining. "The deliverances of our credulity disposition are innocent until proved guilty, not guilty until proved innocent."[34]

Maybe so. But, then, children raised among unreligious people may well disbelieve much that other children quite naturally accept from their believing community. Do Christians and other believers really want to counsel inquirers to cling to their disbelief until they run into irresistible evidence and argument to the contrary? Since Plantinga and Wolterstorff think very little of proofs for bare theism, let alone proofs of the truth of Christianity, why on their principles should anyone move from atheism or agnosticism to accept any religion?

Something in the doctrine clearly must be adjusted or elaborated. For our part, however, it is perhaps best to turn our attention to a different approach to the problem. We have been given what may well be the ablest defense of unargued religious belief in this century, but we need more than that. Our main problem remains unsolved. We want to know not only how the innocently acquired belief of the young and the unphilosophic may be morally justified, but how religious belief can be justified for mature believers alive to the inconclusiveness of the evidence and the objections of the unbelievers.

IV. Newman and the Duty to Believe

In the course of forty years of writing on the topic of religious belief, Newman provided many responses to our central question, some of them very long and very complex. In private correspondence, however, Newman would make his points simply and directly. A response to Mrs. Catherine Ward, composed late in life, fourteen years after the first appearance of the *Grammar of Assent*, delivers his best thought in a few sentences. Though couched in terms of the difficulties of Catholic belief, the object of Mrs. Ward's inquiry, Newman's reply obviously applies to revealed religion as such:

> Reason does not prove that Catholicism is *true* as it proved that mathematical conclusions are true . . . but it proves that there is a *case* for it so strong that we see we ought to accept it. There may be many difficulties which we cannot answer, but still we see on the whole that grounds are sufficient for conviction. This is not the same thing as conviction. If conviction were unavoidable, we might be said to be forced to believe as we are forced to mathematical conclusions, but while there is enough evidence for conviction, whether we *will* be convinced or not, rests with ourselves. . . .
>
> *You can believe what you will*; the only question is whether your reason tells you that you *ought* to believe . . . .[35]

I take Newman to be asserting the following. We are to ask not whether the evidence is adequate to prove a given proposition *P*, but whether it is adequate to warrant the judgment *I am obliged to believe P*. The difference between the two seems clear enough. We all can recall times when we felt that, though we did not understand, say, a proof of a theorem in mathematics, we had plenty of evidence to ground the belief that it was true. Reason insufficient to prove a proposition often suffices to ground the practical judgment that one has an obligation to believe it. This, Newman thinks, is exactly the condition of certain individuals with respect to religious belief.

That it is, or at least can be, needs to be shown. Though neither the letter nor the *Grammar* offers an explicitly formulated argument for the thesis, the *Grammar* provides a wealth of valuable materials for setting one out. The crucial point, easily lost sight of amid detailed psychological considerations, is Newman's extension of Aristotle's doctrine of *phronesis*. Newman notes that in the *Nicomachean Ethics* Aristotle speaks of *phronesis* "as being generally concerned with contingent matter, or what I have called the concrete; . . . he does not treat of it in that work in its general relation to truth and the affirmation of truth, but only as it bears upon *tà praktá*. But there is no reason not to extend the doctrine to cover affirmation of truth." Believing is acting, and the choice to believe is therefore properly subject to guidance by an acquired habit, formed and matured by practice and experience. If in general it is the task of the virtue of *phronesis* to determine "what is to be done now, by this given person, under these circumstances," then it is also the task of that habit of mind to determine when this or that is to be believed by this given person under particular circumstances. The personal act of believing is not to be assessed by norms extraneous to practical reasoning. Excellent practical judgment is open to all the truth the mind can furnish, but it does not expect more than can be required for action. The wise, Newman observes, follow the precept of the *Nicomachean Ethics* to expect exactness in every class of subject according as the nature of the thing admits. As in mathematics we are justified by the dictate of nature in withholding our assent from an undemonstrated conclusion, so by a like dictate we are not justified, in practical matters, especially of religious inquiry, in waiting till such logical demonstration is ours, but are "bound in conscience to seek truth and to look for certainty by modes of proof, which when reduced to the shape of formal propositions, fail to satisfy the severe requisitions of science." So the personal act of believing may well express the excellent practical judgment of a mind that sees enough of the evidence to realize it would be wrong to refuse to honor a divine truth.[36]

And so, while acknowledging the role and importance of evidence, Newman nonetheless insists that it only be evidence and reason adequate for the individual here and now, not strict proof.

If this is right, then proposition (2), the Proportionality Precept, is incorrect as it stands. As Locke and his followers would have it, the precept requires us to ascertain the propriety of believing with a certain degree of confidence by measuring the accepted *proposition* against the available evidence for its truth. The probability of proposition P on evidence E is such and such, and so correspondingly the strength of the belief should be such and such. Newman more properly measures the propriety of the *act* of believing. The act of believing, like any other act, is to be executed if the available evidence is such that one is warranted in believing there is an obligation to perform the act. In effect Newman thus offers an emendation of (2):

(2*) Evidence and reason should be sufficient to warrant the judgment that one ought to believe.

But (1) and (2*) do not entail the conclusion sought by the defender of the *a priori argument*. For though unqualified religious assent is disproportionate to the evidence in the sense that the individual is certain about a proposition inconclusively grounded by evidence, (2*) requires only that enough evidence be available to warrant a decision to act. And of course religious believers think they have such evidence.

The point can be put more positively in the form of an argument that accords, I believe, with the thrust of Newman's thought:

(4) A person has an obligation to do action A if that individual has adequate reason to judge that an end E is personally obligatory and action A is indispensable to E.

(5) It is possible that a person have adequate reason to judge that believing a certain religious proposition is such an A for such an E.

From which follows:

(6) It is possible for a person to have an obligation to believe a certain religious proposition.

The conclusion clearly follows, and it contradicts the conclusion of the *a priori argument* that religious belief is necessarily immoral. What about the truth of the premises?

Proposition (4) certainly seems correct. Mrs. Ward, for example, has an obligation to feed her young children. On the assumption that she had adequate reason to judge that keeping her children healthy as far as was within her power was obligatory, and that she couldn't meet this obligation without feeding them, she would have the obligation to provide them with food and water.

It is of paramount importance to keep in mind that "adequate evidence" does not mean strict proof. Mrs. Ward need not have the most compelling evidence that these are indeed her children, nor need she have a moral theory about the grounds of obligation to know she has the obligation to feed her children. Were that to be insisted upon, few would have any obligations at all.

Certainly, for reasons analogous to those given earlier, the proponent of the *a priori argument* ought to be slow to insist that there is no obligation where there is no apodictic proof of the obligation. For, absent apodictic argument on behalf of the Proportionality Principle, no one has the obligation to equate belief to evidence.

So much, then, for (4). What about (5)?

Could Catherine Ward or anyone else have adequate evidence to know believing was obligatory? Well, why not? Recall, reason may establish an obligation without providing a demonstration. If, then, undemonstrative reason can oblige Mrs. Ward to feed her children, why can't undemonstrative reason oblige her to another kind of action--believing that something is so?

It seems that there are indeed several ways that undemonstrative reason may do just that. One may be brought out by considering the following situation. Having entered an abandond mine without the knowledge or permission of the owners, I find myself suddenly shut off from the entrance by the collapse of the ceilings both in front of and behind me. It is quite obvious that the oxygen left to me will last only a very short time. As I search in the dark for a way out, I see--or think I see--the faintest line of light passing through what may be a thin passage leading up and out, and I hear--I think I hear--a voice above calling down to me. I have no proof, of course, that by trying to crawl up through the one passage available to me I would not be disappointed or would not find myself wedged in a tight space. But what choice do I have? I am bound to try the only passage out. And quickly, for I don't have forever to wait for conclusive evidence.

Similarly, one may reason, I am morally obliged to seek any honorable means to avert the catastrophe posed by my mortality. Christianity represents itself as my only hope to transform the evil of death and the greater tragedy of my own sin. I see--or think I see--a Light. I hear--or think I hear--a Voice. Am I not bound to follow where they lead without waiting until it is too late?

Analogies always limp. In the case of the cave I needn't *believe* that there is a way out; I need only act in hope. In the case of religion, believing itself is the obligatory action, necessary to the life of devotion and commanded by God. Still, the cases are in principle the same. In each I have an obligation to do something because I have adequate reason to judge that an end is obligatory and action indispensable to it. Adequate reason, not proof.

The task for the proponent of the *a priori argument* is a formidable one. It won't do just to attack the analogy or the illustrative end. He must instead show that in *no* case can the believer have adequate reason to judge an act of assent to be necessary to achieve an obligatory end. Moreover it will not suffice to prove (if it can be proved) that the end is not obligatory, the means not indispensable. A believer could be wrong about these matters, just as Mrs. Ward could be wrong in her judgments about her obligations to the children. (These may not in fact be Mrs. Ward's children; this may be poison, not good food, etc.) What an opponent of religious belief must show is that no religious person can possibly *have enough evidence to judge* religious belief to be indispensable to this *or any other end* perceived as obligatory. But a believer may have any number of reasons for thinking that faith is an indispensable condition for any number of indispensable ends. He may reason, not from a supposed obligation to avoid personal destruction, but from the obligation to make restitution and amends for past wrongdoing against self, neighbor, or God. How could it be shown that no one could have good reason to believe this? How could it be shown that no one could have good reason to believe that, where the order of justice cannot be restored by the sinner acting alone, all can nonetheless be made right by the God who bids the repentant sinner to place the matter in His hands? But to begin to examine the evidence is to abandon the *a priori argument*.

"You can believe what you *will*; the only question is whether your reason tells you that you *ought* to believe . . . ." This is indeed the only question. Reason is not to be slighted, we must look for evidence. We are not talking about making Pascal's smart wager[37] or about building up confidence with nothing to go on, like James' man poised to leap over a chasm. Nor are we talking about just sticking to our guns because we were brought up to think about these matters in a certain way. Evidence counts. There's a truth in the Proportionality Precept that must be acknowledged. Ordinarily confidence should match the evidence. Complete confidence in absence of conclusive reasoning is warranted in religious matters because the evidence grounds the judgment that firm belief is obligatory. With God's grace, this is what one comes to see.

The proponent of the *a priori argument* may deny there is or can be evidence adequate even to ground the judgment of obligation. He may contend that neither the existence and splendor of a radically contingent universe, nor the testimony of

Adequate Evidence 93

prophets, apostles, and martyrs, nor miracles, nor the transforming power of the gospel and sacraments, nor the felt presence of God in prayer, nor the nobility and consistency of doctrine, count for anything at all. He may see nothing in the claim that the evidence of the truth offered us grows as we enter more deeply into Christian life, that evidence opens up to us, leaving us convinced that, though it is the nature of the case that there will always be difficulties, a thousand difficulties will not warrant a single doubt. What others see he may not see. Newman writes:

> The Word of Life is offered to a man; and being offered, he has Faith in it. Why? On these two grounds--the word of its human meessenger, and the likelihood of the message. And why does he feel the message probable? Because he has love for it . . . . He has a keen sense of the intrinsic excellence of the message, of its desirableness, of its likeness to what it seems to him Divine Goodness would vouchsafe, did He vouchsafe any."[38]

The unbeliever may be unmoved and unconvinced. But he cannot by *a priori argument* deny religious belief to the rest of us. With us he will have to weigh the evidence.

College of St. Thomas

St. Paul, Minnesota

NOTES

1. *An Essay in Aid of a Grammar of Assent* was first published by Longmans, Green, and Co., London, in 1870. The most recent edition is I. T. Ker's (Oxford: Clarendon Press, 1985). Ker preserves the pagination of the 1889 Longmans' edition, the last Newman saw through press. I quote Ker's edition, but follow the 1889 pagination. References in the paragraph are to pages 162 and 159. (Hereafter references will be abbreviated *Gram.*)

2. Of particular interest are *Fifteen Sermons Preached before the University of Oxford*, published in 1843; *Parochial and Plain Sermons*, 1834-1843;*Apologia Pro Vita Sua*; and *Essay on the development of Christian Doctrine*.

3. Our focus will be on *Faith and Rationality: Reason and Belief in God.*

4. Kenneth Konyndyk usefully distinguishes a variety of arguments employing a proportionality principle in "Faith and Evidentialism," *Rationality, Religious Belief, and Moral Commitment*, ed. Robert Audi and William J. Wainwright (Ithaca and London: Cornell University Press, 1986) 97-107.

5. Newman, *Gram.*, 162, cites Locke's *Essay*, Bk. IV, C. vii, n. 2.

6. George Mavrodes has an interesting discussion of the topic in his "Belief, Proportionality, and Probability," in *Reason and Decision*, ed. Michael Bradie and Kenneth Sayre (Applied Philosophy Program, Bowling Green, Ohio, 1982).

7. As used here, "unqualified assent" is to be distinguished from the following, which are not necessary for unqualified assent, though they are consistent with it: (a) believing in a necessary truth, (b) being unable to conceive anything occurring to falsify

the proposition believed, (c) knowing the truth of the proposition, and (d) never having uneasy feelings or difficulties with the belief. (a) One can give unqualified assent to a contingent proposition. Alice may be dead certain that Adam loves her, and may even say "It has to be so," without meaning that it could not have been otherwise. She need mean only that she is utterly convinced of the fact. And (b) Alice might easily imagine how certain events would change her mind about whether Adam loved her. The religious believer can also imagine falsifying events. A Catholic can imagine a pope or a council formally denying the divinity of Christ--religious belief is falsifiable in principle--but a Catholic can only *imagine* it; he cannot assent to the proposition that the divinity of Christ may be solemnly denied by the Church. Nor (c) is it inconsistent with unqualified belief to say "For all I know, my belief could be false." Faith is firm conviction in the absence of knowledge; so, for all I *know*, what I believe is false. This just means that what I know does not amount to conclusive evidence for the truth of the proposition I believe. "For all I know I may be wrong" does not entail "I may be wrong." (Compare the remark of a blind person who says "For all I can *see* I may be wrong about having two hands.") And (d), since one may not have utterly conclusive evidence for the most firmly held convictions, difficulties and concomitant feelings may easily arise. The thought that his faith is false may occasionally float through the mind of, or even plague, the believer who resolutely rejects it. But, as Newman observed, ten thousand difficulties do not amount to a doubt any more than ten thousand ponies add up to a horse.

8. *Disputed Questions on Truth*, Q. 12, art. 2.

9. *Institutes*, III, ii, 14.

10. "Belief, Proportionality, and Probability," 64.

11. Plantinga, "Reason and Belief in God," *FR*, 17.

12. "Can Belief in God Be Rational If It Has No Foundations?", *FR*, 136.

13. "Introduction," *FR*, 7.

14. *FR*, 3.

15. Plantinga, *FR*, 59.

16. See William Alston, "Christian Experience and Christian Belief," *FR*, 103-134.

17. Plantinga, *FR*, 77.

18. Plantinga's ascription of foundationalist doctrines to Aquinas, *FR*, 90, is mistaken. St. Thomas does subscribe to the essentials of Aristotle's account of theoretical understanding in the *Posterior Analytics*. And that account requires demonstrations of the not-immediately-evident to bottom in the immediately evident. But nowhere, as far as I know, does Aquinas subscribe to the precept that belief must always be proportioned to evidence, and in many places he denies it. The Proportionality Precept conflicts with Aquinas' position on faith and merit. Faith is meritorious just because the will properly and firmly assents to a nonevident proposition under God's inspiration.

19. *Gram.*, 94-95.

20. A similar theme is developed in William Alston's essay in *FR*.

21. *FR*, 163.

22. *Gram.*, 377.

23. For example, Newman often speaks of faith as proper without reasons and evidence. "Will anyone say that a child or uneducated person may not savingly act on Faith, without being able to produce reason why he so acts? What sufficient view has he of Evidences of Christianity? What logical proof of its divinity? If he has none, Faith, viewed as an internal habit or act, does not depend upon inquiry and examination, but has its own

special basis, whatever that is, as truly as conscience has." *Oxford University Sermons* (London: Longmans, Green, and Co., 1898) 184. And, again: "If the great bulk of serious men believe, not because they have examined evidence, but because they are disposed in a certain way--because they are 'ordained to eternal life'--this must be God's order of things." *Ibid.*, 231-232.

24. Wolterstorff does, however, at one point suggest that belief in God may be obligatory for a person even if it is irrational. *FR*, 177.

25. *FR*, 79.

26. One could wish for a more explicitly drawn distinction, but *FR*, 54, seems to reinforce the notion that "evidence" is to be taken as a kind of proposition.

27. *FR*, 155.

28. The example is Mavrodes', in "Jerusalem and Athens Revisited," *FR*, 199.

29. *FR*, 84.

30. *FR*, 84.

31. *FR*, 67.

32. In his attempt to construct a positive account of rationality, Wolterstoff explicitly abstracts from questions of firmness (*FR*, 158). Plantinga discusses firmness as an ingredient of a noetic structure but, so far as I know, does not directly confront the question of whether, in conflict situations, belief should be proportioned to the evidence. Mavrodes construes both Plantinga and Wolterstorff as probably holding that, while theistic belief can be rationally held without an evidential basis, it is illegitimate to be fully convinced on partial and even substantial evidence (*FR*, 215). I am uncertain about that, but there does

seem to be a marked ambivalence in their attitude toward the Proportionality Precept.

33. Plantinga, "Coherentism and the Evidentialist Objection," *Rationality, Religious Belief, and Moral Commitment*, 113.

34. *FR*, 163.

35. 12 October 1884. *Letters and Diaries of John Henry Newman*, Volume XII, ed. Charles Stephen Dessain (London: Thomas Nelson and Sons Ltd., 1962) 289. The emphases are Newman's. Similarly, Newman writes to Mrs. William Froude, 27 June 1848, p. 228: "I wish you would consider whether you have a right notion how to gain faith. It is, we know, the Gift of God, but I am speaking of it as a human process and attained by human means. Faith then is not a conclusion from premises, but the result of an act of the *will*, following upon a *conviction* that to believe is a *duty*. The simple question you have to ask yourself is, 'Have I a *conviction* that I *ought* to accept the (Roman) Catholic Faith as God's word'?" The emphases are Newman's. The argument of these letters is free of the blemishes of the *Grammar* noted by H. H. Price in his Gifford Lectures, *Belief* (London: Humanities Press, 1969) 130-157.

Newman's argument may derive from Aquinas: "The will, influenced by the movement of the good contained in the divine promise, proposes as worthy of assent something not apparent to natural understanding." *Disputed Questions on Truth*, Q. 14. art. 2.

36. *Gram.*, 353, 414, 412.

37. In his original formulation of the wager Pascal assumes that reason can decide nothing here about the matter; the probabilities are equal. Furthermore, if the wager is reconstructed to allow each person to assign probabilities of possible outcomes, the wager renders rational a decision to believe even if the evidence is *against* Christianity, since the possible gain is infinite.

38. Newman, *Oxford University Sermons*, 203.

SOME CONSIDERATIONS CONCERNING PERCEPTUAL PRACTICE AND CHRISTIAN PRACTICE

Dennis Q. McInerny

This essay constitutes a response to Professor William P. Alston's paper "Christian Experience and Christian Belief" in *Faith and Rationality*.[1] What I want to do here is address myself to certain interesting and provocative questions raised by Professor Alston in his paper, but it seems to me that this can most effectively be done for the possible benefit of a reading audience if that audience has fresh before it a précis of Professor Alston's argument. So, before I embark upon my commentary on that argument I want first to delineate its main contours.

I

Professor Alston, along with the other contributors to *Faith and Rationality* is mainly concerned with showing that Christian belief is rational, or at least that it is not irrational. His tack is to focus his attention upon the actual experiences that ordinary Christians have of their Christianity--what he collects under the designation "Christian practice"--and to argue that those experiences provide the basis for regarding Christian belief as rational. This is the guiding assumption, the main thesis, of his paper, and he states it succinctly in the very first sentence: "I take as my starting point the conviction that somehow what goes on in the experience of leading the Christian life provides some ground for Christian belief, makes some contribution to the rationality of Christian belief."[2]

When Professor Alston argues that Christian experience contributes toward the justification of Christian beliefs,[3] the specific kinds of beliefs he has in mind are what he calls "manifestation beliefs," M-beliefs. He is not especially interested in examining the bearing that Christian experiences may have upon beliefs about, for example, the nature and attributes of God as such,[4] although such beliefs could be presumed to be implied by the M-beliefs and discoverable through them. Positively, M-beliefs refer to "how God's nature and activities manifest themselves in our lives," to "the activity of God in the world."[5] The process would seem to work something like this: Christians, on account of their beliefs, would have certain expectations of how God is going to act in their lives; so, when those expectations are met through the kinds of experiences they actually have, the beliefs will be confirmed by the experiences.[6] The "tough problem" that Professor Alston feels has to be dealt with with respect to this procedure for justifying Christian belief has to do with the very fundamental issue of whether the procedure is acceptable. Are we in fact justified "in conceptualizing our experience in those terms?" And that question leads inevitably to another, of rock-bottom significance: "Does the Christian God really exist, and does He do such things as reveal His will to people, whether to me or to someone else?"[7]

By way of answering these questions Professor Alston embarks upon an elaborate analogy between Christian practice, CP, and perceptual practice, PP; indeed, this analogy might be described as the centerpiece of his paper, around which various particular arguments are built. What is the rationale for introducing this analogy? First of all, we need to understand that by perceptual practice is meant simply those experiences of sense perception by which we conclude to the objective existence of the material world. In other words, we make a move from "I seem to see a log burning" to the belief that, objectively considered, there is such a thing as a burning log. Now, it is just that move that prompts the analogy between Christian practice and perceptual practice, for, to Professor Alston, "it is obvious that this familiar move in the epistemology of sense perception is exactly parallel to the challenge we are considering to the claims of religious experience."[8] In other words, there is a parallel between the move, within PP, from certain kinds of perceptual experiences to beliefs about the way the world is, and, within CP, from certain kinds of Christian experiences to beliefs about God and the way He works in human lifes. Because of the parallel between the two practices, the project that Professor Alston sets for himself is to determine whether we are justified in engaging in both. It is important to note, I think, that Professor Alston does not assume that there are no problems attendant upon the justification of PP, and then, on the basis of that assumption, attempt to justify CP by positively comparing it with another epistemic practice (PP) which is already fully justified. Rather, his tactic is to put the two practices on the same level, where both need to be justified. We cannot take the justification of PP for granted.

Before proceeding with the practical task of determining whether PP and CP are justified, Professor Alston spends some time clearing up what we mean by the concept of justification. This turns out to be a rather nuanced discussion, wherein quite a few qualifications, and qualifications of qualifications, are made. Without minimizing the complexity of the issues dealt with here, I do not think I am distorting his governing ideas concerning the matter of justification in saying that the two pivotal notions are what he calls "normative epistemic justification" and "evaluative epistemic justification." As to the former, "stated most generally, this is the notion of not having violated one's intellectual obligations."[9] In this sense, "being justified is a negative status; it consists in one's behavior not being in violation of the norms."[10] The negative status of this kind of justification is made clear when Professor Alston explains that one is justified in this respect if what one has done is *permitted, allowed,* rather than *required.* Now, what is "evaluative epistemic justification"? "S is justified in the evaluative sense in holding a certain belief provided that the relevant circumstances in which that belief is held are such that the belief is at least likely to be true."[11] The heart of the distinction between these two kinds of justification is that one (the normative) is negative--it tells us that a certain practice is not irrational--and the other (the evaluative) is positive; it tells us that a certain practice is rational, in that it "is a generally reliable practice, one that will in general produce true rather than false beliefs."[12] Put differently, we can say that normative justification is weaker in comparison with evaluative justification.

Next Professor Alston turns to the matter of the actual determination of the justification of PP and CP. His general conclusion about PP is that conclusions drawn from it (e.g., burning logs actually exist) are justified "*unless* there are strong reasons to the contrary, unless there are *defeaters* of sufficient strength."[13] In other words, PP is justifiable in the sense that we do not have "sufficient reasons for regarding it as unreliable."[14] Now, as is apparent, that is but negative justification; by drawing conclusions about the way the world is from our sense experiences we are not violating an intellectual obligation. But can we make a stronger case for PP? Can we claim that it is positively reliable? It would seem not, according to Professor Alston. The best we can do for PP is to say we have no good reason for thinking it unreliable. But this is enough to warrant our taking it to be a rational practice.

If that is the judgment on the justification of PP, what are we to say about CP? Here too the assessment is the same. We cannot show CP to be positively reliable, without circularity,[15] any more than we could with PP; but of it we can say, as we did of PP, that there are no reasons for regarding it as unreliable. Lest we think that nothing has been gained here in favor of CP, let us recall that the type of justification that obtains, though weak, is to be taken as warranting rationality. The upshot of this, for Professor Alston, is that CP is "in just the same epistemic position as PP and other commonly accepted basic epistemic practices; and it will be just as rational to take Christian experience to provide *prima facie* justification for M-beliefs as it is to take sense experience to provide *prima facie* justification for perceptual beliefs."[16] If I am rational, on the basis of my seeming to see a burning log in the fireplace, in believing that there *is* a burning log, and a fireplace, then I am no less rational, on the basis of certain experiences I have as a Christian, in believing that God is working providentially in my life.

But perhaps we are being precipitous in supposing that the two, PP and CP, are really on the same plane. Is it not true that there are important differences between the two--for example, and most obviously, PP is pervasive and CP is not--and that these differences count for more than any points of comparison? With the challenge posed by that question in mind, Professor Alston looks closer at CP, wondering if it is indeed justifiable in the sense that we have no reasons for considering it unreliable. Specifically, he considers the argument that CP is not epistemically justifiable because it lacks certain critical characteristics that apply to PP. These characteristics can be summed up by saying that they provide for PP the means for establishing empirical verifiability for its claims. For example, one of the characteristics attributed to PP is that we can check "the accuracy of any particular perceptual belief." Another of the characteristics, already alluded to, is that the capacity for PP, the actual practice itself, "is found universally among normal adult human beings."[17] It would appear that, if the lack of these characteristics in CP forces us to withdraw our previously established judgment that CP is justifiable because there is no reason for considering it unreliable, "then that lack will have to constitute an adequate reason for regarding CP as unreliable."[18]

Professor Alston meets this difficulty in two ways. First, he argues that, although these characteristis are rightly attributable to PP, they do not show that practice to be positively reliable. The most they do is "*manifest* or *evince*[19] reliability," and this is so because of the unavoidable circularity involved in the way the reliability that is claimed for PP is verified: the reliability of PP is shown by adverting to PP. So, we are back where we were formerly. It is not a matter of a positively reliable PP versus a positively unreliable CP, but rather a not-unreliable PP and a not-unreliable CP. They are both in the same boat, epistemically speaking. Professor Alston's second reaction to this difficulty is to wonder about the epistemic potency of the characteristics in question. Granted that CP lacks these characteristics, is that to be taken as a devastating blow against the possibility of justifying CP? "Why should we suppose," Professor Alston asks, "that the lack of these features indicates unreliability?"[20] In fact, he thinks that there is no reason at all to make such a supposition. He returns to a closer examination of the four characteristics, and comes away with the conclusion that they do not stand as necessary conditions for a reliable epistemic practice. This being the case, the fact that CP lacks them does not count against the epistemic reliability of CP.

If throughout the greater part of his paper Professor Alston is more concerned to look at PP and CP as parallel phenomena, at the very end of the paper he takes a sharp turn in direction and there stresses how radically different the two are in terms of the objects of the knowledge of each. "The reality CP claims to put us in touch with is conceived to be vastly different from the physical environment."[21] This being so, "why suppose that the distinctive features of PP set an appropriate standard for the cognitive approach to God?"[22] Professor Alston then delineates certain peculiarities about the nature of God and of religious experience--e.g. God is wholly "other;" hence the human mind cannot "grasp any regularities in His behavior"--with the intention of driving home the point that is incorporated into that question.[23] The general point is this: what works for PP does not work for CP, and this fact is not prejudicial to the latter.

We return yet once again to the acknowledgment that PP and CP have in common that neither can be proven to be positively reliable as epistemic practices. But Professor Alston wants to make yet another effort to link them up to the benefit of CP. Can it not be said that CP "proves itself" in the way PP does? But how does PP prove itself? It does so "with its payoffs of prediction and control of the cause of events."[24] PP provides us with a "map" of the physical and social environment that enables us to find our way around in it.[25] And how does CP--analogously?--"prove itself"? It does so "insofar as it enables the individual to transform himself, or to be transformed, in ways that when they occur will be seen by the individual as supremely fulfilling, as the actualization of his real nature, as what God had planned for him."[26] Another epistemological practice, "interpersonal perception" (i.e., the awareness of other persons as persons), is briefly introduced by way of setting the stage for the theme on which the paper ends. We are told that this particular practice "can no more be justified from the outside than any of the others we have been considering."[27] So it is "internal self-justification"[28] that presumably we have been concerned with all along. And, with respect to CP in particular, the point is made explicitly that its justification "cannot be decided except from the inside."[29]

II

As mentioned, the analogy Professor Alston establishes between PP and CP forms the centerpiece of his paper, and most of the weight of his argument for the rationality of Christian belief rests upon that analogy. We have noted his contention that there is an exact parallel between (a) the "familiar move" made in PP from having certain perceptions and believing certain things are objectively so, and, in Christian practice, (b) the move from having certain Christian experiences and believing certain things to be true about God acting in the world. But are these two sets of circumstances exactly parallel? While not denying there are similarities between the two, we should not ignore some salient dissimilarities, the most significant of which would be the positioning of belief within each practice and showing how it colors the nature of the practice itself.

What I mean is this: with respect to CP, belief is constitutive of the practice itself, whereas this is not the case with respect to perceptual practice. To put the point more plainly: In order to accept the reading of Christian experiences as confirmatory of how God deals with His people I must already be possessed of Christian belief. It is as if, in CP, Christian experience is bracketed by belief. Belief precedes, and belief follows upon, the experience. One must have Christian belief in the first instance, before one can have Christian experience; so, one cannot engage in CP without Christian belief. This is what I mean when I say that it is constitutive of the practice. In order for the practice to come into play at all one must be possessed of a certain belief. Now, I do not see this to be the case with respect to PP. The very possibility of my engaging in PP does not depend, as far as I can see, upon the antecedent possession of a belief of a certain kind--an epistemological belief, let us say--or of any belief whatsoever. Unlike CP, in which there are conditions which must be met before it is put into play, there is something of the automatic about PP; it is put into play willy-nilly. One need not formulate any theory about what the world is and how it works in order to make the "familiar move" that people habitually make regarding their perceptions. But let us be more precise about the matter, in order to establish the contrast between PP and CP more clearly. One need not be a conscious, committed adherent of a specific epistemological world view in order to be established within PP at all. But that is just what is needed in order to be established within CP. And that stands as no mean difference between PP and CP.

With those considerations in mind, let us return to Professor Alston's point that there is an exact parallel between the moves made in PP and CP. At first glance this might seem to be just the case, but only, I would suggest, if one focuses on the moves themselves and ignores the contexts in which each takes place, where the contexts are altogether important. So, it is true that there is a parallel between any perceiver, on the basis of his perceptions, arriving at certain judgments about the nature of the world, and any Christian, on the basis of his Christian experiences, arriving at certain judgments about the way God deals with His creatures. But in order to see those two moves as significantly similar we need to view them in isolation from the conditions upon which they depend. However, the conditions of each are so different so as to make the moves themselves, despite surface likenesses, to be, I would argue, themselves significantly different. The condition for CP, as we have seen, is Christian belief--we could without exaggeration call belief a *sine qua non* condition of the practice--whereas the condition for PP is simply rational sentience.

"Rational sentience" is not the most felicitous of terms. All I mean by it is the capacity for the five basic kinds of sensation which are possessed by human beings. The requirements for involvement in PP, then, are what we might call minimal. One is qualified for the practice simply by reason of one's status as a human being. Additionally, and in contrast to the requirements for CP, those for PP are non-ideological. By speaking specifically of *rational* sentience, I am not implying that any conscious intellectual position need be taken with respect to any epistemological theory; by that qualifier I simply intend to call attention to the fact that the sentience in question here is that of a rational creature, and will therefore, inevitably, be colored accordingly. Admission to CP, on the other hand, requires the assumption of an ideological stance. One must first adopt a conscious point of view;[30] then and only then does one become a practitioner.

Let us spell out yet more explicitly the practical ramifications of the two kinds of conditions upon which PP and CP respectively depend. Because one's status as a human being is sufficient to admit one to PP, the category of those who engage in perceptual practice is a large one; in fact, it is coterminous with the category of human being. This is obviously not the case with respect to CP. Here, to be admitted to the practice, it is not enough simply to be a human being. Here one must be a specific sort of human being, a human being with a certain set of religious convictions. Now, the number of this specific sort of human being, relative to the entire category, is small. Professor Alston asserts that we should not allow ourselves to be prejudiced against CP simply because, in contrast to PP, it is engaged in by relatively few. That point is well taken, but it seems that it is not a question of the relatively small numbers who engage in CP, but rather the question of whether the "move" made within that practice is truly comparable to the "move" made within PP.

It would appear that it is not. Apart from the differences already delineated, I would argue that the two moves are fundamentally disanalogous and that that is so principally on account of the two quite different functions they perform. Stated briefly, the function of the PP move is to establish, whereas the function of the CP move is to confirm. Let us consider first CP. Professor Alston more than once calls our attention to the essentially confirmatory effect of the kinds of experiences had by one engaged in CP.[31] In explicit terms this is how it works: by reason of being a Christian believer I am enabled to engage in CP. Central to that practice is my having my original beliefs confirmed ("reinforced," the sociologist would no doubt say) by actual experiences that I have. Let us say that one of the particular Christian beliefs to which I adhere is that God will reveal His will to His people. Let us say further that I find myself at a certain point in my life where I am seriously confused over an important issue. A critical decision needs to be made, but I am not at all sure *how* it should be made. In due course, I see my way clear toward making the decision in a certain way. In the aftermath of making the decision I am possessed of a calm assurance that I decided correctly, that I did the right thing. Now, the interpretation I place upon this experience is that God revealed His will to me in this important matter, and that I have followed His will. But it is important to note what this experience does *not* do: it is not productive of a certain belief about how God acts toward His people. It simply bolsters up a belief that is already in place, and, if that particular Christian belief were not adhered to by an individual--an atheist, say--then the type of experience described would be open to many alternate interpretations. That is to say, generally the same type of experience could be confirmatory of a wide variety of beliefs. Indeed, it would appear that virtually any type of belief could be confirmed by a "move" of this sort, for what is confirmed by the practice is that which constitutes the practice. What you enter with is what you exit with.

But is it not the case that something quite different from this is going on in PP? First of all, as we have seen, one does not need to be the adherent of any kind of epistemological belief in order to engage in PP. More importantly, while it is quite possible that PP can have a confirmatory effect,[32] this is by no means its key characteristic, as is the case with CP. CP, in order to be CP, must confirm; but PP is not defined by its confirmatory effects. And we can say more: that PP is *productive* of beliefs concerning matters epistemological. Whereas, with CP, we have to be committed to a set of conceptions about the way the world is in order for that practice even to work, we need no such presuppositions to trigger PP and the move which, I would say, is naturally made within it. The judgment that there are objectively existent burning logs follows upon perception; it is produced by perception. The objectifying move is not the ratification of a theory, but an intellectual judgment of the sort around which theories are built.

In sum, the differences that obtain between the move of PP and the move of CP are pronounced enough that we do not appear to have a very sound basis for considering them to be exactly parallel. Fundamentally by reason of the diverse ends to which they are oriented they are quite different moves.

III

Let us alter our perspective now and look at PP and CP from the point of view of the kinds of knowledge with which respectively they deal. And let us begin by recalling the kind of activity going on within each practice. In the case of PP we have a subject who is experiencing certain sense perceptions: he is having the experience of seeing a log burning, as well as, let us say--to flesh out the picture a bit--the experience of smelling a log burning. On the basis of the experience he concludes that burning logs exist. We can say he has knowledge of the actual existence of burning logs. If we ask him how he knows that burning logs actually exist, he tells us: "Because I see them; I smell them." His knowledge, he is confident, is of the way the world is, of what in fact obtains, of reality. And that knowledge is founded upon the exercise of a natural ability of his. Actually, to call it a natural ability does not come nearly close enough to describing something which is in fact so integral to the nature of our subject that it is part of the definition of what he is. Sensation is indicative not so much of what man has as of what he is. Man is a sensing being. So, we can say that the kind of knowledge in question here is of a most fundamental kind because it rests upon the very mode of man's being. Man has knowledge of this kind because he is sensate and present in the world.

How are the circumstances with respect to a subject engaged in CP? What is going on here? We begin by noting that the Christian has certain kinds of experiences, and those experiences, as we know, serve to confirm his Christian beliefs. This must mean that those experiences have for a subject a certain demonstrative force; they act as grounds that support his beliefs. But let us look at those experiences more closely. Are they on a par with the kind of experiences which our subject engaged in PP has? There the experiences are simply sensations--seeing and smelling. But is that the case with the experiences of the subject engaged in CP? It would seem not. Here the subject is not using what we might call brute sensation as the basis for making judgments about the way the world is. The Christian, we can assume, has quite made up his mind about how the world is--he acknowledges the objective existence of things. So, although the experience at issue here necessarily involves sensation, it would seem to be considerably more than brute sensation. It is what we might call interpreted sensation. Now, because it perhaps could be argued that all sensation is interpreted, let us call this ideologically interpreted sensation, in contradistinction to epistemologically interpreted sensation. But there is no reason to stall over fancy terminology. What I mean to say is that the sensation which is part of the experience of the Christian engaged in CP is informed with meaning in a way that is not the case when it is a matter of seeing or smelling a burning log. From those sensations a subject takes one step to the judgment that burning logs exist. If a Christian hears a voice, in response to that sensation he takes the step common to all human beings and concludes things like: there is someone out here; that someone is speaking to me; that someone is Anastasius. But, insofar as he is engaged in CP, he takes a second step as well, acknowledging, simply by taking the step, that his sensations are freighted with special significance. He makes the determination that what Anastasius is saying to him now, at an hour of profound crisis in his life, is a manifestation of God's love and providential care for him.

What is the nature of the Christian's knowledge in this circumstance? In the first place, we can say that with regard to the first step he makes--from hearing something to the judgment that there is someone speaking to him--there is no difference between the Christian's knowledge and the knowledge of any person engaged in PP; he is simply knowing *qua* human being. But with regard to the second step there is something quite distinctive about the knowledge of the Christian. It is based only secondarily on sensation--or, if you will, more broadly, on the way he is naturally constituted. It is based primarily on something not endemic to his nature, something which is superimposed upon his nature and which is his by reason of a purely gratuitous donation: his faith.

If we were to query the Christian about his knowledge, he might respond to us by saying, "I know that God providentially watches over me and sees me through difficult times." And if we were to ask him how he knows things like this he would reply by saying that he has certain experiences that ground such knowledge. And he may tell us about what Anastasius had said to him on a certain critical occasion. But what is it that really founds his knowledge, justifies it? Certainly it is not simply experiences themselves, such as being the auditor of words spoken by Anastasius, for it is notoriously common that a believer and non-believer can have the same experiences, which have the effect on one of confirming his faith and quite a different effect on the other. What really founds the Christian's knowledge is his faith. This is to say that the kind of knowledge--specifically Christian knowledge--which is possessed by the Christian *qua* Christian is radically different from the kind of knowledge possessed by the human perceiver *qua* human perceiver, from the point of view of what each, ultimately, is based upon. We could put it this way: in order to know that burning logs objectively exist, I need not in any direct, practical way depend upon anyone beside myself; on the other hand, in order to know that God providentially guides my ways I must of necessity depend upon God. The knowledge of the believer finds justification only secondarily in life's experiences; ultimately, his confidence in what he knows finds its source in the transcendent.

It seems to me that, precisely because of the radically different kinds of knowledge that are operative within PP and CP--we could provide a shorthand indication of the difference by calling them simply natural and supernatural knowledge--an additional strain is put upon Professor Alston's analogy between PP and CP.

IV

In the first section of this essay we say that Professor Alston, in order to make a stronger case for his analogy, analyzes four features which, the argument goes, are possessed by PP but which are lacking to CP. (See note 17.) Professor Alston concedes the basic point, admitting that CP indeed lacks these four features. Now, what these features purportedly show is that PP is epistemologically reliable. On that account, PP and CP would appear to be critically disanalogous for, if CP is lacking the features, then presumably it is not epistemologically reliable. This conclusion is blocked, we recall, by Professor Alston's assertion that the four features in question are not to be considered as necessary for reliability. Professor Alston scrutinizes the four features with the intention of showing how they cannot stand as necessary conditions of reliability. His general conclusion about them is that their alleged capability of demonstrating PP to be positively reliable is questionable because there is no non-circular way of showing their effectiveness in this respect. Short of examining his entire critique of the four features, I want at this point to comment on his remarks on one of the features, bearing on observations I have already made in the foregoing discussion.

In response to the fact that the "capacity for PP, and practice of it, is found universally among normal adult human beings," and in the attempt to show that this particular feature is not necessary for reliability, Professor Alston observes that there are certain practices which are obviously respected and whose reliability is not questioned, and which, like CP, also lack this feature. The examples he cites are (a) wine tasting and (b) the kind of aural discrimination required of an orchestra conductor. The argument implied by the observation would seem to run along these lines:

"Those who would argue for the reliability of PP, in contrast specifically with CP, cite as one of the indicators of that reliability the fact that PP is engaged in by all normal adult human beings. We must grant that CP is, obviously, not engaged in by all adult human beings. But does this provide sufficient grounds for our considering it unreliable? It does not. Consider other epistemic practices, such as those engaged in by a wine taster and an orchestra leader. These are respected practices; they are deemed reliable. But is either of them engaged in by anything even remotely approaching the totality of adult human beings? Not at all, and this fact is not held against them; it does not count against their reliability. So, the fact that CP is not engaged in by the totality of adult human beings should not be held as counting against its reliability."

Professor Alston's argument has a certain surface appeal to it, but beneath its surface I detect some problems that, again, have the effect of unsettling the analogical balance upon which the argument depends. If the argument is going to work, then there would have to be some salient commonality between CP, on the one hand, and the practice of wine tasting and orchestra leading, on the other hand. If that were not the case, Professor Alston would find himself in the position of committing essentially the same type of fallacy he cites when he cautions us not to be quick about attributing reliability to PP simply because it is engaged in by many; we should not succumb to what he describes as the "big is good" mentality.[33] If CP, wine tasting, and orchestra leading have no more in common than the fact that they are engaged in by relatively few (although CP would constitute a mega-category in comparison with either wine tasting or orchestra leading), and if that is the only fact we are calling attention to by way of substantiating their reliability, then we would be falling into a fallacy characterized by the "small is good" mentality; we could be accused, perhaps, of subscribing to a kind of epistemological elitism. So, it is not the relative smallness of the numbers of their practitioners which allows us to compare CP with wine tasting and orchestra leading. What, then, is it?

In attempting to answer that question I think we shall find that CP in fact stands in a pronouncedly disanalogous position with respect to both wine tasting and orchestra leading, and the reason for this is, once again, traceable back to the fact that what is in question is two radically different kinds of knowledge. What differentiates me from the wine taster? We are both capable of tasting wine in the more elementary sense. I take a sip of California chablis; he takes a sip of California chablis. We are both tasting California chablis. What differentiates us is that his taste is educated; it can make discriminations, some of them quite subtle, whereas mine cannot. And he ends by making a judgment about the wine. He declares, let us say, "This chablis is superb." And a like situation obtains with respect to me and the orchestra leader. Both of us hear the performance of Beethoven's Seventh Symphony, but his hearing it is quite different from my hearing it, and that is because his knowledge is different from, and better than, mine. And in the aftermath of the hearing, whereas I am apt to enthuse indiscriminately, he comes forward with a whole complex of highly nuanced judgments about the performance.

Now, what is especially noteworthy about the judgments made by the wine taster and the orchestra leader is that the knowledge upon which those judgments rest proceeds from their respective experiences themselves. The virtues of wine tasting and orchestra leading are brought into being and perfected by the actual practice of them. But, as we have seen, this is not so with CP. The Christian is not brought to the point where he can say "In this instance God has clearly revealed His will to me" simply by reason of certain activities he engages in. The faith knowledge of the Christian is not determined by human experience; it determines human experience. It bursts in upon human experience, and transforms it.

CP, on the one hand, and wine tasting and orchestra leading, on the other, are critically dissimilar epistemic practices. Hence, it would seem that not much could be said, positively or negatively, about the reliability of the former by comparing it with the latter.

V

Toward the end of his paper Professor Alston introduces a new dimension to his analogous treatment of PP and CP. Seeing only seemingly insurmountable difficulties in the way of proving either PP or CP to be reliable "from the outside," as it were, he asks us to consider that the reliability of both might rest upon the ability of both to "prove themselves." In other words, just as PP proves itself, so it can be seen that CP too proves itself.

Let us remind ourselves of what we learned in the first section of this essay, that to say that PP proves itself means that it demonstrates its reliability with its "payoffs of prediction and control of the cause of events," and by enabling us to find our way around in the physical and social environment. Refreshing our memory further, we recall that CP proves itself "insofar as it enables the individual to transform himself, or to be transformed, in ways that when they occur will be seen by the individual as supremely fulfilling, as the actualization of his real nature, as what God had planned for him." It would seem, on the face of it, that what "proving itself" amounts to, as evinced by either PP or CP, is that, from the point of view of the participants of each, each can be seen to work. In the case of PP this pragmatic quality of its indicators is clearly in evidence. PP proves itself because it allows me to function effectively in the world. More precisely, I suppose, this means, among other things, that PP proves itself by everywhere ratifying my judgment that material things objectively exist. I am moving about, not within my own head only, but within the world.

If we look to what counts for "proving itself" with regard to CP, there we find, besides the obvious pragmatic slant, that the tonality here is decidedly moral, and this in contrast with the predominantly epistemological tonality within PP. PP proves itself because the practitioner, *as is*, is enabled to make his way in the world. CP, on the other hand, proves itself by altering the subject himself, indeed, by transforming him. Again, in this contrast we can see the radical difference that exists between PP and CP. In fact, so marked is this difference that it seems odd to talk of CP proving itself at all. In any event, it does not seem to do so as PP proves itself, where proving itself seems to be tantamount to a ratification of the *activities* constitutive of PP itself. In other words, there is a certain compelling quality to the notion of "proving itself" as applied to this practice. But with CP it is not, it can never be, an "inside job." It is not, ultimately, the activity he engages in that transforms the Christian, but rather the grace of God.

But, those considerations aside, I must say that I am puzzled by the very notion of an epistemological practice proving itself, as Professor Alston develops the notion. I would like to call attention to two problems, one particular and one general, that attend his development of this notion. We have seen immediately above that PP is said to prove itself because of, among other things, its predictive payoffs. Now, I fully agree that the fact that we are capable of making predictions about the world in which we live argues strongly for the reliability of PP, but I am a bit confused when I hear Professor Alston argue this way, for, in his analysis of the four features conventionally attributed to PP, among which features was the predictive capacity of that practice, his task was to show that these features were not necessary conditions for reliability. Does that mean that predictive capacity, specifically, is dispensable, not all that important? But, if that is so, why cite it as a key demonstrative characteristic of a practice proving itself?

On a more general level, Professor Alston concedes the point that a good case cannot be made for either PP or CP being positively reliable. And the concession is made on the basis that any attempt to show either of the practices to be reliable in any strong, positive sense would involve circular argumentation. But now, by introducing the notion of a practice "proving itself," Professor Alston very much seems to be wanting us to accept both PP and CP as in fact reliable in a strong, positive sense. But how else can this be--the notion of "proving itself" speaks for itself in this regard--except by circular argumentation?

VI

Professor Alston's notion of an epistemological practice proving itself is closely allied with another notion which we called attention to in the first section of this essay, and which serves, it seems, as the point to which his entire paper is leading--the notion of epistemological "internal self-justification." We saw that what this means, as far as CP specifically is concerned, is that the justification of the practice "cannot be decided except from the inside." In other words, CP proves itself.

The general point here is clear enough but, when we look closely at what is being asserted, certain obscurities present themselves. The first thing that needs to be determined is the extension of the term "inside." Is reference being made to the individual person, or to a collection of persons, in this case, the Christian community? If it is the case of the former, then what is being advocated, of course, is a rather intense form of subjectivism. It is a matter of the individual Christian having satisfied himself that certain of his experiences are in fact corroborative of his beliefs. The decision about this is made "from the inside"; understood, there is a way in which it could not be otherwise. But to what extent are the criteria on the basis of which the decision is made also "inside"? If we were to suppose that they are entirely so, then it is easy to see the kinds of problems that any individual could be faced with. One recalls the benighted protagonist of Charles Brocken Brown's novel *Wieland* who was internally self-justified, we could say, in his belief that God had commanded him to slaughter members of his own family. He was convinced in his own mind not only that what he was doing was right but that, by doing it, he was following the will of God as explicitly manifested to him. Now, the truth of the matter is that Wieland was mad, but a simple judgment of that sort carries no weight whatsoever if justification is purely subjective. Now, despite some ambiguities in his treatment of internal self-justification at the end of his paper, Professor Alston would not advocate an intensely subjective interpretation of the notion; we are better advised, therefore, to regard the "inside" in question here as relating to the Christian community. In just a moment I shall turn to a consideration of that possibility, but first I want to extend my analysis of the subjective interpretation of internal self-justification a bit further.

If internal self-justification were entirely subjective, how would CP prove itself? Focusing our question more sharply, we might ask "What kind of movement would constitute the proof?" If, for example, a Christian is certain that God has revealed His will to him in a given circumstance, this would presumably mean that his peculiarly Christian experiences, which are such because of his Christian belief, have had the effect of confirming his Christian belief. Certainly there is a tight circularity here. Indeed, this circumstance would seem to be hermetically sealed, and virtually impenetrable from the outside. What could possibly count against it, except what would be regarded as intrusive exterior criteria? Whatever contributions to internal coherency, to the establishment of a kind of epistemological equanimity, a process of this kind might provide, I do not think it has much to do with proof in any serious sense of the word. There must needs be a public dimension to proof; indeed, that is integral to its operation so that, even when I say such things as "George proves something to himself," what is being referred to is George's apparent success in squaring the private realm with the public; the subjective with the objective.

Let us now consider the "inside" as pertaining to the Christian community. If we should assert, with Professor Alston, that Christian practice can be justified only from the inside, this consideration then releases us from the difficulties of subjectivism. In this circumstance, the Christian is not completely on his own. He can rely on other Christians to help him out as he interprets his own experiences. And if, as in the case of Wieland, he comes up with an egregiously wrong notion of what God wants of him, there will be conscientious fellow Christians at his side to correct his errors and guide him aright. It is just that particular type of situation which raises an interesting question. It is fairly easy to see how a Christian might be confirmed in his belief at any given time. George is inclined to acknowledge that following a certain course of action is in fact the will of God for him. After consulting with his confessor and several other fellow Christians, George is confirmed in his belief. We can appreciate that this kind of justification is indeed an "internal" affair, and we can hardly expect the non-Christian to attach much weight to the very experiences which, for George, carry strong confirmatory force. But now let us ask this: is it possible to be dis-confirmed within the Christian community? I think we can respond affirmatively to that question. A Christian may have a mistaken belief about what constitutes the will of God in a given instance, and he can have that belief dis-confirmed by fellow Christians, as, unfortunately, did not happen with Wieland.

We might imagine a Christian who conceives it to be the will of God for him that he blow up the UNESCO building in Paris because it has been revealed to him that that is a diabolical organiation. Happily, before he does anything rash, he is convinced by fellow Christians to whom he reveals his plan that such an act would be thoroughly un-Christian, and that to claim it could be the will of God would be a gross contradiction, a blasphemy. They succeed in dis-confirming his belief by appealing to various Christian principles; in other words, the criteria on the basis of which the putative act is judged wrong would be "internal." But the interesting thing about a situation of this kind is that one would not need to be an insider, i.e., a Christian, either to see the wrongness of the act, or, even possibly, to be able to persuade the would-be perpetrator of the act not to go through with it, on the basis of principles other than Christian principles, i.e., of non-"internal" criteria. It is not inconceivable that an atheist could succeed in dis-confirming the belief of the would-be bomber. His success, of course, would not depend on his efforts to show the act could not possibly be the will of God; rather, he would probably argue that the act was inhuman, or irrational, or perhaps simply impractical. What is being appealed to in the Christian by the atheist is not his Christian conscience but, for want of a better term, what we might call simply his human conscience. Now, let us consider again the possibility that our would-be bomber was dis-confirmed in his belief by fellow Christians. Is it reasonable to suppose that they succeeded in their task by appealing to purely Christian criteria (i.e., purely "inside" criteria)? Is there anything logically to preclude the possibility that they also appealed to criteria that any level-headed outsider could appreciate as fitting for the circumstance and, for the insider, argumentatively compelling? An atheist, say, looking in on the situation, would be able to see and acknowledge the legitimacy of both the dis-confirming *and* the confirming procedure. He would not, as an atheist, be able to accept certain data (e.g., assertions of a Christian about the significance of his experience) as grounds confirmatory of Christian belief, but he perceives the import of the relationships that obtain in the operation he is witnessing. In other words, he would be able to see *that* certain data are serving as grounds even though he himself is unable to accept them as grounds--i.e., as carrying confirmatory force. And he probably would be willing to concede that, *if* he did accept the data as grounds, then he would logically be compelled toward accepting what the grounds support. But the general point is that the atheist, as outsider, is able to appreciate the logic of the elementary move that is being made within Christian practice, for that move, from premises to conclusion, is not a peculiarly Christian move. It is a human move. And we might even want to say that the atheist, despite his inability to accept Christian premises, would be willing to accord to Christian practice a kind of purely formal rationality.

The purpose of these reflections is to raise questions about Professor Alston's contention that the justification for Christian belief can be come by exclusively within the ambit of the Christian community and in terms of what we might call Christian criteria. Certainly there is no denying the critical importance of Christian belief for CP; the former is a *sine qua non* condition for the latter. But when the Christian is confirmed in his beliefs through his experiences he is not functioning simply as a Christian--as if there were a peculiarly, even exclusively, Christian way of reasoning--but as a rational creature, following formalities that any rational creature, including non-Christians, would recognize as correct in their basic structures.

VII

Professor Alston's principal intent is to show that Christian belief is rational, in the broadest sense. To show that CP is rational in the broadest sense comes down to this: while you cannot positively demonstrate its rationality, you can at least show that nothing *counts against* its rationality. It is to be assumed innocent until it is proven to be guilty; and it cannot be proven to be guilty. In other words, CP is to be regarded as rational in the respect that it is not irrational. The function of the analogy between PP and CP I take to be generally describable in this fashion: PP is a common practice, a familiar practice; it enjoys practical legitimacy; it is trusted; it would be an odd circumstance were people habitually to question it, to doubt its reliability; now, on the face of it, CP does not enjoy anything like the degree of acceptability that is characteristic of perceptual practice; its reliability is very much open to question. Professor Alston brings together PP and CP to prompt us, in the first instance, to have a closer look at PP. The superficial view would have it that it can be positively shown to be reliable, whereas this is not so with CP, and therefore CP, unlike PP, bears doubtful credentials for rationality. However, that closer look at PP would apprise us of the fact that it really cannot be positively shown to be reliable. So, both practices are the same in that particular respect. What we have, then, is an epistemic practice--PP--which is regarded as rational even though it cannot positively be shown to be reliable. If we compare this practice with CP we should be led, through the comparison, to accept CP also as rational, for it too cannot positively be shown to be reliable. In other words, the basic question is this: if we do not hold against PP the fact that it cannot be epistemologically justified in any strong sense, why should we hold that against CP?

It has been my intention in this essay to call attention to various disanalogous characteristics of PP and CP. These are significant enough, it seems to me, to seriously affect the force of Professor Alston's argument. I do not think we have in the approach he has taken the best way to make a case for the rationality of Christian belief. Let me stress that. My point is certainly not that Christian belief is not rational, nor that it cannot be shown to be rational, but simply that an analogy between PP and CP constitutes a rather cumbersome basis on which to show Christian belief to be rational. It tends to raise more problems than it settles.

The key problem, as I see it, turns on the issue of knowledge. PP and CP deal essentially with two different kinds of knowledge, their difference founded on the difference between the natural and the supernatural orders. Now, it would be doing a disservice to Professor Alston to imply that he does not acknowledge that difference. He does, and in fact takes pains to call attention to it in his paper, stressing that the person engaged in CP participates in a kind of knowledge not accessible to our ordinary means of analysis. But this recognition serves only to put in greater relief the difficulties that hamper the analogy of which so very much is being required.

College of St. Thomas

St. Paul, Minnesota

NOTES

1. Alvin Plantinga and Nicholas Wolterstorff, ed., *Faith and Rationality: Reason and Belief in God* (Notre Dame: University of Notre Dame Press, 1983).

2. *FR*, 103.

3. He does not want to claim too much for Christian experience in this respect. "I am not suggesting that this is the whole ground or that it can do the whole job. I have no aspiration to be the late twentieth-century Schleiermacher, spinning the whole web of Christian doctrine out of the personal experience of the contemporary believer." Ibid.

4. There is, of course, no reason to preclude the possibility that Christian experience could provide the grounds for beliefs about the nature and attributes of God, for Christian experience includes speculative intellectual activity.

5. *FR*, 105.

6. "The Christian beliefs under consideration say that God will manifest Himself in certain ways in our individual or corporate experience. From time to time we find such manifestations in our experience. This provides empirical confirmation for the beliefs in question." Ibid.

7. *FR*, 106-107.

8. *FR*, 108.

9. *FR*, 113.

10. *FR*, 114.

11. *FR*, 115.

12. Ibid.

13. *FR*, 112.

14. *FR*, 116.

15. All he means by this is that any attempt to demonstrate the positive reliability of conceptual practice (or Christian practice) must necessarily rely on perceptual practice (or Christian practice).

16. *FR*, 120.

17. The four characteristics Professor Alston discusses (*FR*, 121) are as follows:

1. Within PP there are standard ways of checking the accuracy of any particular perceptual belief. If, by looking at a cup, I form the belief that there is coffee in it, I can check the belief for accuracy by smelling or tasting the contents; I can get other observers to look at it, smell it, or taste it; I can run chemical tests on it and get other people to do so.

2. By engaging in PP we can discover regularities in the behavior of objects putatively observed, and on this basis we can, to a certain extent, effectively predict the course of events.

3. Capacity for PP, and practice of it, is found universally among normal adult human beings.

4. All normal adult human beings, whatever their culture, use basically the same conceptual scheme in objectifying their sense experience.

18. *FR*, 123.

19. *FR*, 125.

20. *FR*, 124.

21. *FR*, 128.

22. *FR*, 129.

23. All of these features are listed on p. 129.

24. *FR*, 131.

25. Ibid.

26. Ibid.

27. Ibid.

28. Ibid.

29. *FR*, 132.

30. My position here is not that Christian belief is *no more than* a conscious point of view; however, it is that.

31. This is a theme common to Professors Alston, Plantinga, and Wolterstorff. All three call attention to the fact that Christian experiences confirm Christian belief, and that this fact, in turn, is at the heart of the argument for the rationality of Christian belief.

32. I do not want to preclude the obvious possibility that one *can* have certain epistemological beliefs, or an elaborate epistemological theory, which find confirmation in one's perceptual practice. A realist's perception of a burning log confirms his belief that burning logs exist independent of his perceiving them. But whence comes the theory of realism?

33. In this context he speaks of "an egalitarian prejudice in epistemology that would have it that what is not shared by all sorts and conditions of men cannot be the real thing." *FR*, 120.

PRELIMINARIES TO THE FIVE WAYS

Richard J. Connell

I

A. Introductory remarks

To say that the function of reason in relation to Faith has been debated for centuries is to say what everyone knows, and our own times continue to see the issues discussed. Recently a volume of essays has been published[1] in which a number of writers--who in the main defend the Continental Reformed (Calvinist) tradition--discuss the relation between Faith and reason, focusing particularly on the proposition "God exists." Historically, discussions of this issue have tended to center around the arguments for God's existence, and since medieval times attention has been centered on the arguments known as the Five Ways that appear in the *Summa Theologiae* of Thomas Aquinas. It is interesting to note, however, that the editors and principal writers, Plantinga and Wolterstorff, make no allusion to those proofs that bears directly on the efficacy or character of the arguments themselves. Now one might well wonder why that is until he reads the essays, at which time he understands that what these authors consider the function of reason to be in relation to Faith has little in common with the relation of reason to Faith that is part of the background for the Five Ways. P. and W. consider these arguments to depend on what they call "classical foundationalism," an epistemological position they reject, which means that the Five Ways can have little bearing on what P. and W. consider the role of reason to be in relation to believing that God exists. The rational acceptance of the proposition "God exists" does not, in their eyes, require articulating and understanding proofs.

It would seem that the gap between P. and W. on the one hand and Aquinas on the other is a consequence of some misconceptions about a number of things, many of which are dealt with in other essays in this volume. A principal one appears to be the distinction between the medieval understanding of the character of Christian belief in the proposition "God exists" and the assent to that same proposition generated by an efficacious proof (assuming there is one) containing the proposition as a conclusion. Yet, over and beyond that particular difference, it seems that there are other difficulties which are philosophical in character and which stem from misunderstandings about the proofs themselves. In what follows, I shall address myself as well as I am able to making clear some of those misunderstandings, taking the position of P. and W. as the starting point for the first of my comments. Later, other topics will be aired because a larger number than the writers in *Faith and Rationality* appear not to take account of them.

B. The general plan of the essay

My aim in the following is to consider four main issues, each with its own subconsiderations. The main issues are the following: (1) the kind of "basic propositions" upon which the Five Ways depend; (2) the empirical character of those propositions; (3) the general educational background presupposed by the Five Ways; (4) the description of certain empirically established causal correlations that are presupposed by the arguments; (5) some considerations on causes of motion; (6) some distinctions that are preliminary to an understanding of the Five Ways; (6) the order among the proofs and the relation of that order to the empirical character of the entire argumentative procedure represented by the Five Ways. Before we begin to discuss the issues, however, I wish to make some general remarks about the proofs as they are presented in the *Summa*, for there is a widespread failure to understand that those arguments are not complete as they stand. After that I wish to describe in a general way the intellectual predisposition required for the arguments, but I do not assume my remarks to be directed to every reader.

C. Some General Comments on the Five Ways

The five ways as presented in the *Summa* are only sketches, a claim readily verified by those who are familiar with the points Aquinas himself makes about causes in a number of places. The first way alone occupies the last two books of Aristotle's *Physica*, books which are devoted essentially to an elaboration of the first way and which talk about many things not treated in the *Summa*. Obviously, then, the few lines devoted to the first way cannot recapitulate all that is discussed in the *Physica*.

The second way, which superficially resembles the first, requires many considerations on agent causes that Aquinas takes up in several contexts, and which are omitted from the proof as it is presented in the *Summa*.

As for the third way, the difficulties connected with the proposition *omne corruptible aliquando corrumpitur* are considerable. Aristotle defends it at length in his *De Caelo et Mundo*,[2] but what he does there and what Aquinas adds in his commentary on Aristotle appear not to be taken into account. That, it would seem, is an important reason why the third way is misunderstood, and why it is regarded as inefficacious. Furthermore, the "cosmological argument" as presented by Kant is an inaccurate representation of the first three ways, and Kant would seem to be the main reason for the lacunae in modern conceptions of what the arguments attempt to do.

To illustrate the sort of misunderstanding that comes from considering only the sketches that appear in the *Summa*, consider the following passage:

As I noted above, there are two major objections to the crucial step (ii) in Aquinas's argument for (2). First, it does not seem to be universally true that if one thing causes a second thing to change toward a certain state, the first thing must actually be in that state. It does seem true that if something makes water become hot, it must itself be hot. But suppose a plant is in a process of dying. Must that which causes the plant to be changing toward the state of being dead be something that itself is already actually dead? Moreover, doesn't Aquinas believe that God can directly cause cold water to become hot? But it makes no sense to say that God is in the state of being hot. Perhaps Aquinas only meant to assert that if one thing causes a second thing to be changing toward a certain state, the first thing must actually be in that state or have all that that state represents in another form. Thus, although God is not actually hot, He has all the power that is represented by the state of heat. However, once we begin to qualify Aquinas's basic principle in this way, the principle becomes vague to a degree that renders it difficult to understand exactly what is being asserted and it becomes less clear that a thing cannot cause a change to take place in itself.[3]

To anyone familiar with the works of Aquinas, the above passage is readily seen to result from a failure to read anything more than the arguments in the *Summa*. It exhibits an absence of even a rudimentary acquaintance with Aquinas' considerations connected with the notions of agent and moving causes. So, having made the foregoing general remarks, let us now turn to the issues themselves.

D. The Preparatory Disposition required for the Five Ways

To begin, let us note that historically the first proposals put forward as causal accounts of nature were myths, which present metaphorical accounts of gods who are said to be responsible for the many categories of things and phenomena we observe. The gods are described as movers, that is, as causes of physical changes such as storms, earthquakes, etc., and as agents which are causes of entities, for example, the various kinds of animals. Roughly speaking, there is one deity-cause for every category of animal or, perhaps more generally, for each category of entity and phenomenon that provokes men to wonder.

Augustine, who borrowed from Varro, says that myths are not all alike, maintaining that they are of three kinds: the myths of the politicians, the myths of the poets, and the myths of the academicians. Unfortunately, Augustine notes, myths get corrupted, and it is hard to determine their original forms. Politicians like to turn religion to purely political ends, and poets find that myths make good stories; only the myths of the philosophers, he says, are uncorrupted by extraneous desires. They alone, then, are worthy of comment.

We can all see that mythical explanations of natural phenomena are not proposed without experience and observation; for arguments by analogy, upon which myths are founded, do not originate in a vacuum. Ordinary experience reveals that the universe is a kind of whole that has an order within it, however much the whole and the relations of its parts to one another are only confusedly, only indeterminately, understood. To understand in an imperfect way that the universe is one thing we do not need to be cosmologists. Moreover, the ordered-thing universe is an effect which suggests not only the existence of gods but also their hierarchical ordering. Mythologies commonly postulate a first, principal god who in one way or another dominates the others; a God of gods is common.[4] Furthermore, I understand from an authority that, even when a pantheon is recognized, the religion that is lived, the religion that has a cult, is a religion of one god. The lived religion tends to be monolatrous.[5]

In this connection it is interesting to note that according to Jean Piaget[6] young children do not recognize the distinction between the natural and the artificial but, when at an older age they finally do, they tend to describe man-like entities as causes of nature. We ought not, however, to find such behavior strange; for human agents are the first causes of which children have experience,[7] and that gods should be conceived of after a human image is to be expected. It would seem, then, that there is a basic disposition to believe in the existence of God, a disposition that appears, however, to be the consequence of the normal functioning of the intelligence and not a "natural instinct" that somehow presents God as existing without a rational--in the sense of argumentative--grounding.

But we do not wish to make too much of the existence of myths; for they certainly do not establish apodictically that God exists. Nonetheless they do play an important, preparatory role in our coming to understand God, and they ought not to be overlooked. It would seem that in a general, confused way myths are sufficiently reasonable to require arguments to the contrary if they are to be denied, which allows us to say that an atheistic attitude is unnatural in the sense that the mind's first overview of nature inclines it to accept the existence of gods as causes rather than to think that the universe is independent of everything outside itself. An assumption of atheism, when compared to these first, probable convictions, is unreasonable; for it goes against the available evidence and does so without argument. However, we have come to the end of our introductory remarks, and we are now ready to consider the main issues that we outlined earlier.

II

E. "Basic Propositions"

In discussing what is meant by a "basic proposition" Plantinga, and Wolterstorff too, assumes without discussion that the issue bears on what is basic for some individual person, and that what is basic for one is not basic for another. And the rational, they think, varies from one person to the next; for it is a function of an individual's experience, his subjective dispositions, his moral status, and other singular traits, habits, inclinations, etc., that go to distinguish individuals from one another. As Wolterstorff puts it, "rationality is person specific and situation specific." Plantinga reduces this point to its simplest expression when, speaking of what it is for a person to be rational, he says:

> . . . the irrational is the impermissible, the rational is the permissible.

That sort of criterion would never have been accepted by Aquinas or other Aristotelians. Aquinas used "reason" first of all as the name of a kind of intelligence--the human--that had to make use of a discursive movement by which it went from what it already knew to something initially obscure, in such a way that what was initially known provided a light for what subsequently came to be known. In short, "reason" was a name for an intelligence that went from premises to conclusion; hence "rational" (at least in the Aristotelian context) can hardly escape the notion of argument; and, even if absolutely first starting points cannot themselves be the result of (deductive) argumentation, they are, nonetheless, preliminaries to it. Furthermore, when the issues pertain to some systematic discipline, then the inquiry is essentially rational because even the starting-points, the first propositions, are premises and hence parts of arguments. Also, systematic procedures, particularly those which have to do with the most difficult and obscure issues, must be regulated in a stringent fashion by the canons of logic. One of the reasons natural theology has been regarded as intrinsically difficult is its requirement of absolutely strict objectivity; that is, the natural theologian must leave aside his private inclinations, dispositions, etc., which of course is a task we all find difficult. More importantly, to the extent that such subjective dispositions are determinative of an intellectual position, to that extent the position is not rational in any strict sense. (We omit here the matter of Revelation, for reasons that are considered in another essay.)

For P. and W., evidence is also to be construed as pertaining to individuals. In discussing self-evident propositions Plantinga remarks that

> this notion must be relativized to *persons*; what is self-evident to you might not be to me.

Now to consider *basic proposition, rationality,* and *evidence* only to the extent that they are individuated in different persons is to put oneself at the opposite end of the epistemological universe from Aquinas and Aristotle when it comes to talking about the proposition "God exists." The position of Aquinas is that this proposition is a conclusion of an argument that is the fruit of a systematic investigation of some considerable length and difficulty; and, like every systematic, scientific investigation, its domain of inquiry is confined to that which is limited by general propositions. In other words, every systematic inquiry, insofar as it seeks to show why something is so, or that it is so, or what it is--every such inquiry is confined to the level of universals, of classes; and it is concerned with individuals only to the extent that they represent what is common to the category, genus, species, or other class. To be interested in individuals as such, to be interested in what is peculiar to individuals, requires the application of universal principles, to be sure; but, over and beyond the principles, such considerations must take into account the circumstances unique to each. But that, Aquinas (and other Aristotelians) would say, is not a concern in this sort of issue.

As a consequence, when one limits his consideration to regularities, to general propositions connecting universals, the notion of *per se notum* or *self-evident* pertains to what is intrinsic to the proposition itself. A proposition that is *per se notum* is one in which upon analysis the predicate is seen to belong to the definition of the subject. Now some propositions, Aquinas would say, can be recognized as such by every normally functioning adult, and they usually are, even if the adults cannot point to the propositions in a reflective way. On that account the propositions are *per se nota* for everyone. Other such statements are not so amenable to analysis. They are more difficult to see and require reflection, consideration, and even argumentation, to be recognized for what they are. But as long as the connection between subject and predicate is not directly proved by a demonstrative argument, as long as the arguments are extrinsic to the propositions, the latter qualify, if true and necessary, as analytic, as *per se nota*.[8] As Aquinas uses it, the latter phrase cannot be translated as "evident to the senses"; it cannot be rendered as "obvious," for that is not at all its sense as it is employed in medieval philosophy. Many propositions that are verifiable only by observation could never be taken as "self-evident" as that word translates *per se nota*, an example of which is the statement "Fido is brown."

Thus, it is not surprising that Plantinga and Wolterstorff should make little reference to Aquinas except to criticize him. They seek to render an account of *basic proposition, rationality,* and *evidence* that could never be a part of what Aquinas does. The Five Ways are not addressed to Everyman but only to the sophisticated. Obviously they are not intended to be a part of a simple evangelizing process.

F. Empirical Regularities: General Considerations

In addition to starting from first principles which are general, a systematic procedure that seeks ultimately to conclude to God's existence must also start from propositions that are empirical, from propositions that are founded on observation.[9] To put the point in a contemporary vocabulary, Aquinas held that the basic propositions of systematic considerations--whether those we now call "scientific" or those we call "philosophical"--must start from facts. In our day, as well as his, every systematic consideration worthy of the name considers itself tied to the facts both for is starting-points and for its ultimate standard of measure; so what "fact" means and what the ordinary usage of the term implies is worth examining.

Originally "fact" came into English from the Latin "factum," which means "that which is done or made and has been achieved or finished." *Webster's* (II) lists the English cognate as having a sense similar to the original: "a thing done, a deed." Another dictionary gives the first meaning of fact as "something that actually exists or has actually occurred; something known by observation or experience to be true or real: a scientific fact." This is the primary sense of the term as it is employed in scientific considerations, and the point of importance is that when it is used in this way the word signifies something observable.

But there is another sense of the term closely related to the first, according to which "fact" can signify--*Webster's* tells us--"an occurrence, quality, or relation, the reality of which is manifest in experience or may be *inferred* [emphasis supplied] with certainty." The emphasis is for the sake of stressing that ordinary experience regards as obvious our ability to infer unobservable realities from those that are observable; and the arguments for God's existence depend upon that ability. Indeed, the dependence of the mind on observation and the mind's need to infer unobservable causes and effects from facts, from observables, is fundamental to Aquinas' procedures, as we shall see later. But, to repeat what we have already said: the proofs are not open to Everyman; for, though the arguments are ultimately founded on empirical regularities, the latter are not recognized as premisses of arguments by any but the intellectually sophisticated precisely because they must be reflectively appreciated and systematically ordered. Of course just how empirical regularities are employed and just how they supply necessary principles are matters requiring too much discussion for the limited space here.

It is plain, however, that the first principles cannot be hypotheses. On the contrary, the world is an *effect* from which one comes to know its causes. More specifically, the universe taken as *one effect*--the formality necessary to prove that God exists--cannot have anything extrinsic to it which would allow for a "prediction" from an hypothesis that would confirm or disconfirm such an assumption. And, without such a confirmation, there is no hypothesis in any proper sense of the term; only a scientifically empty locution.

G. The empirical background for systematic investigations

Preliminaries to the Five Ways 139

The kind of ordinary experience that provides causal myths with a limited cogency can be the starting point for arguments concluding to a first mover, provided that ordinary experience is subjected to a systematic examination regulated by determinate methodological principles. And, though in principle ordinary experience suffices, I would add that it is greatly aided by the observational regularities modern science makes available. Such vicarious experience is especially important today for those of us who, living in modern cities, usually do not acquire by ourselves even the common observational regularities upon which the arguments depend. Moreover, since the human intelligence can come to an understanding of unobservable realities (things unseen, as St. Paul says) only through an examination and analysis of natural entities (things seen), an examination of the world of nature must be made with care.

In contrast with our own state of affairs, it is interesting to consider the reflections of John Wilson, who, speaking of the American Indian, says:

> He is to be a hunter and an inhabitant of the woods. Now, imagine all the multitude of natural facts, on the knowledge of which, for safety and sustenance, his mind is made to rest. He is a hunter--that is to say that, from the day he can use his hands at his will, he will begin his warfare against the animal race. What does that mean? That, of every bird and animal of which his power can compass the destruction, he must begin to know the signs, the haunts, the ways. He is already engaged as an observer in natural history. You may be sure he has very soon as exact a knowledge of the figure, colours, cries, etc., of many of them, and of the place and construction of the habitations of those which find, or make themselves, habitations--of their young, or eggs--their number, their seasons, and precautions of breeding, etc., as any naturalist from Linnaeus to Cuvier. . . . I ask, is it not

plain that he must possess, very intimately and exactly, much of that knowledge which, when possessed by a naturalist, is raised to the rank of science?[10]

And this store of learning, this soaking in regularities, was valuable not solely for practical ends; on the contrary, it inevitably led to the contemplation of a first cause, with whom Indian culture was familiar.

Described more determinately, what I have said about the experiential background required for an understanding of the Five Ways means, as far as systematically considered regularities are concerned, (1) that we must be familiar with the substance of Aristotle's *Physica* and the issues it treats; and (2) that we ought to have that kind of educational acquaintance with other natural disciplines which produces the educated man, as he is described by Aristotle:

> Every systematic science, the humblest and the noblest alike, seems to admit of two distinct kinds of proficiency, one of which may be properly called scientific knowledge of the subject, while the other is a kind of educational acquaintance with it. For an educated man should be able to form a fair off-hand judgment as to the goodness or badness of the method used by a professor in his exposition. To be educated is in fact to be able to do this; and even the man of universal education we deem to be such in virtue of his having this ability. It will, however, of course, be understood that we only ascribe universal education to one who in his own individual person is thus critical in all or nearly all branches of knowledge, and not to one who has a like ability merely in some special subject. For it is possible for man to have this competence in some one branch of knowledge without having it in all.[11]

Although one who wishes to understand the proofs must be educated according to Aristotle's description, nonetheless not all the sciences and arts are relevant to the arguments in the same way, and not all are equally important. Some disciplines are relevant as providing an observational groundwork supplementing the ordinary experience from which the proofs' conclusions are drawn, while others contribute to the development of the educated man without being directly related to the theoretical issues of the arguments. In regard to the disciplines which provide a groundwork, one ought to have some physics (including a little astronomy), some chemistry, and some biology, though he certainly need not be an expert. Up to a point, of course, the more one knows of those sciences the better; but essentially he needs only a common understanding of the notions relevant to the considerations of natural philosophy, together with an exposure to the evidence that provokes the formulation of the principal scientific hypotheses. Not the least advantage to be had is a kind of habitual accumulation of experience, of regularities, which serves to fasten the intelligence to nature, a state of affairs that is foreign to that philosophy which wishes to start with an epistemology or with "phenomena," that is, with internal, subjective states, or which merely follows some current, faddish, philosophical "figure." It is not false to say that the proofs can make their case with us only after we have "soaked" to some extent in the relevant natural phenomena. (I am told that Aristotle classified the organisms of the Aegean Sea and its surroundings before he wrote his *Categories*, which is an abstract, logical treatise; and, whether that is true or not, it is a wise way to go about such a business.) Such, then, would seem to be the general dispositional and educational background required for the Five Ways; and once again we see that they are not addressed to Everyman but only to the sophisticated.

H. Some Common Regularities and some Empirically Ascertained Causal Relations presupposed by the Five Ways

First let us note some regularities pertaining to the kinds of motion--continuous changes--that occur in nature and the relations they bear to one another. Local motion, as well as other physical changes (principally heating and changes of state, together with the concomitant alteration of properties which are secondary effects of changes of state), all bear a determinate relation to one another. When we consider nature as an ordered whole, we see determinate relations among entities and their changes. Animals depend on plants for their food; plants depend on carbon dioxide together with sunlight to manufacture the materials of which they are made; chemical changes for their occurrence depend on variations in equilibrium conditions, principally solar heating; the effectiveness of solar heating depends on the position of the earth's surface relative to the sun, which of course is a function of the rotation and revolution of the earth, both of which are local motions. And all weather phenomena--upon which climate and growing conditions depend--are the result of the unequal distribution of heat energy in the atmosphere, which in turn results from the relative inclination of the earth's axis to the plane of revolution. That affects the amount of incident sunlight per unit area of the earth's surface as the earth moves in its orbit. Thus, nature's serially related changes lead back to the motion of the earth in relation to the sun as the first motion in the ordered series, which allows us to say that local motion is *causal* in relation to physical, chemical, and biological changes.

This point is important, since the argument for a first mover in nature can now be seen to bear on a cause that is responsible for local motion, which according to modern cosmological theories is itself responsible for the formation of the celestial bodies through the expansion of the cosmological "atom" that results from the "spreading out" of photons and particles, the expansion in turn causing the cooling of the universe and the formation of stable elements. But, returning to the time of Aquinas, we can see that it is no accident that in his first way he gives the motion of the sun as an example. According to his cosmology, the mover of the sun is the physically unmoved mover of natural motions.

There is still another point to be made before we leave behind these regularities, and it has to do with ancient notions of the sun as a god, as a manifestation of a deity. Ordinary experience, even without the refinements of modern science, suffices to show the dependence of natural phenomena on the sun; it suffices to show that there is a certain universal dependence of nature on solar radiation. On that account, then, because of the sun's general causal role in nature, we ought not to be surprised to see it deified. Observation does show that in some way it is a kind of first cause, and that is what the name "god" means: a cause that is first, at least in some order, if not absolutely. Furthermore, the understanding of the Sun-God of some ancient civilizations, notably the Egyptian, was sophisticated. Their religion was monotheistic; their God was just, a creator, etc. In short, it seems that, as soon as the mind recognizes certain fundamental causal relations, it "leaps the gap," so to speak, on the basis of its imperfect grasp of the causes in nature, and of the unreasonableness of an infinite series.

I. Causes of motion

Aristotle and his commentators understood that movements or motions are the key to understanding the constitutions and principles of things. Were everything in nature perfectly static or fixed, we could know only those distinctions that are directly observable; all others would escape us. On that account, then, we argue to the existence of unobservable causes, whether internal or external to things, on the basis of the behavior that entities exhibit. For instance, the movement of a compass needle, an acceleration of a celestial body, a rise in temperature, all require an accounting. The reason for this of course, is that properties do not bring themselves into existence, and neither do things. We correlate a "source of energy," as the physicist would call it, with the coming to be of the property or thing. Such correlations are regularities that function as starting points for causal considerations of changes in nature. And we might ask: what sort of world would we have if properties and things brought themselves into existence? An unintelligible world, to be sure.[12]

Furthermore, it is this causal relation that permits the mind to move from observables to unobservables. Plainly, if an observable at one time shows only itself to the intelligence and at some other time points to something unobservable, it follows that the observable (or a correlation it bears to some other observable) is somehow different the second time; and the possible differences are three: the observable can come into existence, pass out of existence, or undergo a variation within itself. An increase in pulse rate indicates an infection, or possibly excitement; a moving compass needle a magnetic field; an acceleration in a planet the presence of a source of gravity, etc. And the principle involved is known by people of the most primitive societies. They recognize unobservable causes through variations in observable traits; and, though they do not articulate the proposition, they know that properties do not bring themselves into existence or bring about variations in themselves.

But, if it is the case that everyone is able to recognize that properties neither vary themselves nor come into existence by themselves, then we must indeed be dealing with a *basic proposition*, and one that is basic for every normally functioning man. Nor is its character difficult to come by. If, for instance, a billiard ball is lying on the table, or a stone on the ground, we all understand that if it is to move it must receive its motion from an outside source and, when we understand that, it is because in the background we assent to the proposition "Whatever is received (acquired) is received (acquired) from another." This proposition is indeed intelligible from its own subject and predicate; for, as soon as we understand the notions of *receiving* and *another*, we see the proposition to be true. Moreover, its negative counterpart is equally intelligible: "Nothing can communicate to itself what it does not have." And of course, when something begins to exist or undergoes a variation, it receives something. What it did not originally have is communicated to it. In short, the causal relation is indeed basic; the mind encounters it in the observable traits that are the first realities we know, and it is understood by Everyman. Even for evangelization, such a proposition is required; for God is not naturally intelligible to us except as a cause.

It is interesting to note, too, that when we argue from an observable motion to an unobservable cause--for instance, from an acceleration to an unobserved gravitational source--we do not instantly ask about or look for an infinite series of causes.

However much one must discuss infinite series in the arguments for God's existence, the natural inclination of the intelligence is to assume that there must be something which is first.

Thus, when changes occur in nature or when things come to be, we are able to correlate a cause with them, even though the cause may be unobservable.[13] We are able to argue by induction to the proposition: whatever comes to be comes to be from a cause that is distinct from what comes to be. We see this proposition verified in the coming to be of artefacts, of organisms; we see it in chemical changes (the elements act on one another) and in physical changes. So we may quote the medievals: *omne quod movetur ab alio movetur.* But we must not go too far; for, although the induction establishes this proposition as a regularity, the induction does not include every one of the movements in nature. It does not include the cause of that local motion which is first, the movements of the celestial bodies in Aristotle's day, the motion of photons in our own, motions of both of which the causes are unobservable. One might think that photons are self-moving, that their motion is unreceived; and, if he does, he raises a problem that can be answered only by the kind of apodictic argument Aristotle offers in his *Physica.*

J. Some Necessary and Basic Systematic Distinctions

Modern philosophy has abandoned using the distinction between substance and property (accident) in most of its considerations, even when the distinction is admitted as legitimate. One is reminded of Aristotle's criticism of Anaxagoras, who postulated God as a kind of first cause, but once having done so never used Him as a principle of explanation. So, too, the contemporary recognition of substance is without use, and the consequence is that the Five Ways cannot be seen in their true cogency, a point that needs some elaboration.

The distinction Aristotle made between substance and property is necessary for philosophy first of all to ground a category theory; for the relation of the categories to one another is wholly arbitrary without it. If substance is abandoned and there are no natural categories, then every reality is on a par with every other, and none is a principle of order with respect to the rest. In such a "world," chance would determine "kinds" of things, motions would not require a subject, and so would be substantive; and perhaps a Marxist theory of internal contradictions would be a way to account for motion and development.

Beyond its use for category theory, the substance-property distinction is also necessary to justify the number and character of the proofs, because that which is a cause of a physical change, a change of property, is not, *as such*, capable of being a cause of the production of a substance. This is an important proposition for Aristotelian causal theory, and it suggests an order among the proofs. But, before we take up that issue, let us first look at how modern science assumes the truth of a principle that is but a more specific form of a general proposition about moving and agent causes.

K. A *per se notum* Causal Principle from the Natural Sciences

If one asks the simple question "What do I need in order to raise the temperature of a flask of distilled water from 0 degrees Celsius to 100 degrees Celsius?" the answer is not hard to provide. If one uses a source of heat, his source must be at the temperature of 100 degrees or more; it cannot be at 50 degrees, 75 degrees, or even at 99.999999 degrees. (The difference plainly can become too small to measure, but that is not relevant.) Furthermore, if we have a liter of water and attempt to boil it by inserting a pin that is red hot, we still shall not succeed, although the temperature of the pin is well above 100 degrees Celsius. And the reason once more is plain: despite the temperature, the quantity of heat in the pin is inadequate to achieve the desired effect. But now what all this means in philosophic terms is that *the agent or mover must be proportioned to the effect to be achieved.*[14]

Let it be noted, too, that the proportion between mover and moved, especially evident in the example above, is between the mover (the source of heat) and the *primary* effect. The secondary effects of heating are several: the viscous becomes less viscous as it becomes warmer; the conductive less conductive; the hard, soft. And, when philosophers say that the effect comes to resemble the cause, the statement is made in regard to the primary effect. One can use a battery to heat a solution that contains an electrolyte, but the primary or immediate effect of the battery is to electrify the solution; only as a secondary effect does the solution become hot.

Nor is it necessary that the mover or agent resemble the effect in a univocal manner. An engineer who designs a machine does not physically resemble the machine, but the design in his head is certainly a likeness of that which is produced. On that account, then, God does not have to be hot in order to make water become hot. As for the dead being produced by the dead, the error here is more fundamental. The dead as such is a non-entity and certainly cannot act. But more importantly--in a sense--death is a kind of change that is called "destruction" or "corruption," and it is always the consequence of a production or generation. When an animal dies, fertilizer is produced. We call this kind of change a "destruction" or "corruption" whenever the posterior entity, the new one that comes to be, is inferior to that which existed before. Correspondingly, when that which comes to be is superior to the antecedent from which it came to be, we call the process a "production" or "generation."

Similar arguments can be put forward to show that a mechanical agent must be proportioned to the acceleration it is to produce, and to show the need for a proportion between an electromagnetic cause and its proper effect. Furthermore, if one claims that there is no need to have a source of heat that is equivalent to or greater than 100 degrees in order to boil a flask of water (or that a force must be proportioned to its acceleration), then he will effectively claim (to use the physicist's words) that energy can be created, denying thereby the first law of thermodynamics, without which physics and chemistry fall.

Continuing the same topic, to say that a moving or agent cause must be proportioned to its effect is to say what the Aristotelians like to put in another way: *a moving or agent cause can act only in the measure that it is actual*; that is, the cause can act only to the extent that it possesses--not necessarily in the same mode, as we said above--that which comes to be in the effect. Put negatively, to say that a mover or agent can produce an effect not antecedently in the mover or agent is equivalent to saying that the agent can act *qua non-being*, which amounts to holding that something can come to be from nothing as from an agent cause.[15] The first law of thermodynamics is but a more contracted statement of that philosophic principle. But now to our last topic.

L. The Order among the Arguments

Although this section will discuss the order among the arguments by grounding itself on the formalities proper to each of the Five Ways, there is a general reason for their order that can be given in advance: it has to do with their differing proximity to sensation. The various kinds of continuous change that are here called motion are observable; hence they are directly apprehended by the sensory powers and are most intelligible to us. But physical substances are not observable, and so they must be known through their observable properties, especially through their operations. On that account, substances are less intelligible to us, though they are inherently more intelligible than properties, which is to say that intrinsically there is more to substances than there is to properties. Immaterial substances, on the other hand, are not subjects of observable properties, which means that our knowing them depends on our having previously come to understand substances that do have observable properties.

Now at this point it is important to note that, when one argues from an effect to its cause, *he cannot come to see anything more in the cause than is contained in the effect*, except that he may deny of the cause the imperfections proper to the effect. Stated in logical terms: the conclusion cannot contain more than is found in the premisses. Consequently, since the effects from which the Five Ways proceed are not ontologically equivalent, it follows that what one sees in the first cause to which an argument leads varies according to the effect from which the argument starts. So, with those general points having been made, let us now consider each of the arguments in turn.

1. *The argument for a first mover.*

Because motions in nature manifest the kind of dependency we discussed earlier when we saw that local motion is causal with respect to the other kinds of continuous change occurring in nature, it becomes plain, for that reason if for no other, that the formality proper to the first way is local motion, which means that the conclusion that can be drawn through the argument is limited to a cause which does not exceed that formality. The first mover may well be God himself; but the first way cannot formally conclude to Him *insofar as the first way depends on physical motion as its starting point.* That is, we do not know much about what the cause is other than that it is an unmoved mover possessing its motive power by itself. Even when we take into account that we cannot have an infinite series of movers, we still know the unmoved mover only to the extent that the effect, physical motion, is capable of revealing its cause. Of course "motion" can be extended to cover intellectual and volitional movements (spiritual motions) but, as depending upon sensations and as thus providing the ground for the first way, "motion" has not been extended to the immaterial realm; therefore it can conclude to an absolutely first cause only in an indeterminate way. "Motion," however, is potentially extendible to cover intellectual motions; and, if the formality is so extended, one has a more powerful argument that reveals more about the first cause. An entity that is incapable either of physical or immaterial motion lacks every potentiality whatsoever; and so it is *actus purus*.

We should note that it is not necessary that God be *directly* responsible for motion, for the latter occurs *in an already existing substance*, and that which is presupposed to any causal action cannot be accounted for by an effect posterior to what is presupposed.[16] In other words, a first *physical* mover can presuppose existing substances and so could be someone or something other than God, because such a mover can be a cause that is not first absolutely. (We must remember, too, that, prior to the argument for a first mover of physical motion, we have no systematic proof of the existence of a substance outside the realm of nature, which means that we have no grounds for extending the term "motion" beyond the physical realm.) The "unmoved" in "unmoved mover" must first be understood as a privation of *physical motion*. And, because motion is a property convertible with material substance, the unmoved mover cannot be of a material constitution: this has to be the first step of the argument. Then, after one precludes an infinite series, the argument would seem to conclude to God only in an indeterminate way, insofar as it arrives at a first cause that has its power for physical motion from itself and not from another. But again, if "motion" is extended to give a broader formality, the argument becomes more forceful.

The temptation to switch formalities in the first and second ways is illustrated by the words of John of St. Thomas when he discusses the argument for a first mover:

> If however [the mover] is not moved by another mover in that genus [of motion] but is moved by itself, then either it has its power of moving and motion from another or not. If it has the power from another, then one must go back to the argument about an infinite process. But, if it has the power from itself, then, just as it has the power, so it has its essence and its existence from itself, which is to be unproduced and uncreated.[17]

Everything is fine in the lines above until we read "just as it has the power, so it has its essence and its existence from itself, which is to be unproduced and uncreated." At this point, I maintain, John of St. Thomas has switched formalities. To speak of essence and existence, especially as they are understood to belong to the first cause, is to speak under a broader, metaphysical formality. Without adverting specifically to what he has done, it would seem that he has added to the argument for a first mover considerations that do not belong to it.

2. The second way.[18]

The second way is not just another argument for a first mover; instead it is formally an argument to a first *agent*; and the agent cause to which one concludes is a cause which is responsible for material substances--not natural aggregates. When one recognizes substance to be distinct from properties, he realizes that the first way asks for the second way, because motion, in addition to presupposing existing substances, *can be no more than an instrumental cause vis-à-vis the production of substances.* The reason is, of course, that nothing can act beyond its own category except as an instrument directed by a superior cause. Furthermore, since, as we have said, natural substances are produced by actions on preexisting substance-materials, the second way, like the first, does not clearly conclude to God, for the reason that *a cause other than God can produce substanes through operations on preexisting materials.* Apart from man, who requires God's direct action to bring the human soul into existence, a cause other than God could be responsible for natural species. Indeed, it is not impossible even for man to produce a new species of organism; and, were he to do so, he plainly would not be the kind of agent that is involved in ordinary reproduction, whereby a new individual of the species is brought to be by another individual of the same kind. On the contrary, man would be the cause of *the species as such.* Thus the cause to which the second way concludes is not an individual, univocal agent, but the kind of agent cause the medievals called "universal." That is the agent Aristotle said his predecessors knew nothing about.

It is necessary to repeat that, because the argument starts from the species of natural substances, it concludes to God only indeterminately, even though He is the first agent. And the reason has already been given: natural substances are brought out of the potentialities of natural materials, which are presupposed to natural generative actions. The argument, therefore, does not account for the preexisting materials and so is not a formality fully proportioned to revealing God as the first cause. The effect from which the argument starts is limited. But, as with the first way, if one extends the formality to include immaterial as well as material substances, the argument concludes to an efficient cause that is responsible for being as such.

Let it not be thought that I do an injustice to Aquinas' position, for in the following text, among others, he lays the groundwork for what I have said:

> However, in every natural thing we find that it is a being [ens], and that it is a natural thing, and that it is of such or such a nature. The first of these is common to all beings; the second to all natural things; the third to one species; and the fourth, if we add accidents, is proper to this individual.[19]

The distinction of formalities is of course well founded and correct; so it would seem that the second way, like the first, falls short of a full manifestation of the first cause.

To expand the point a bit, one should note that it is possible to argue from natural things to a universal agent in two ways. First, by grounding oneself formally on the natures of substances, without supposing anything about their chronological appearance. Individuals account only for the coming-to-be of other individuals, not for the coming-to-be of natures as such, since the individuals already possess these natures. Stated more determinately, the second way accounts for the "design" of the natures of physical sustances, organisms being the most obvious cases. To be the cause of the nature as such of an organism, to account for its design, is to be responsible for the collocation of its operational capacities, together with the modifications which adapt the capacities to one another and which adapt physical properties to the operating organs, according to the demands of the organism's ecological niche, which is to say, to the demands of the mode of living peculiar to the organism.

A second procedure by which one can conclude to a universal agent is by arguing against the spontaneous generation of a first organism in an evolutionary process and/or the appearance of a

Preliminaries to the Five Ways 153

succession of superior species-substances. In this case the argument must start from the principle requiring that there be an agent proportioned to the substance-effect, which means that the cause cannot be merely a mover; it must be ontologically adequate to bringing about the effect. This principle denies what is currently held by many, namely, that an antecedent species which is operationally inferior to a posterior species can be the progenitor of the posterior species.[20] To repeat: if an antecedent species is held to be the agent cause of a posterior but superior substance-species, the only causal relation the first can have to the second is that of instrumental agent.[21] And, if the antecedent species can be no more than an instrument, then the principal cause, the one actually proportioned to the effect, must be something else that is ouside nature but simultaneously operative. That, I would argue, is the conclusion to be drawn; and the chronological succession of species about which evolution informs us reduces the difficulty of seeing the cogency of the argument for a first agent. One must, of course, first take time to consider the character of chance events in order to show that the production of biological species out of inanimate materials and movers alone is not possible; he must, in other words, have established, by his consideration of substance in nature, the inadequacy of a reductionist, mechanistic position, a position that is presupposed to maintaining that chance alone[22] is the originating cause of species.[23]

Before leaving this issue, let us note that, when Aquinas speaks of the cause of that which is natural in physical substances, we ought to keep in mind that the natural world with which we are familiar is an ordered whole. Ecologists have been at pains to make plain to us our mutual species-dependencies that constitute the ecosystem. On that account, then, because nature is an ordered whole, it is *one effect* and requires one cause to account for that effect. That, it would seem, is part of the justification of the distinction of formalities Aquinas made in the text cited earlier.[24] But now, having made the remarks above about biological species, we must go on to make a point about the need for an agent that is responsible for the realm of the inanimate.

Aristotle considered the motions of heavy and light bodies to be consequent upon their constitutions,[25] which require their mover to be the agent that generated them. In our own day, we posit the motion of photons to follow upon their existence as photons, as a consequence of which an argument for a first mover that is applicable to those fundamentally active constituents of the universe can lead by itself to a mover which is also an agent cause, and a creator at that (assuming that the primordial "fireball" would have to come from nothing and could not be the term of a prior collapse); for the fundamental entities would otherwise have had to come to be from nothing. Aristotle's argument in Book VII of his *Physica*, when put in a modern context, can be directed at showing that even such things as photons, which appear to be self-moving, require to be moved by another; and in all this we suppose, of course, the current cosmological theories which see the universe originating from a big bang.[26]

3. *The third way.*

The third way argues from the distinction between the necessary and the contingent, a distinction which divides that most universal formality, *what exists* (*ens* in Latin or "being" in some English renderings). The contingent, it is argued, cannot exist by itself but depends on something that exists necessarily; hence there must be a necessary first being, which now, for the first time, is fully seen to be God. This formality, I maintain, is proportioned to our seeing God as causing an effect that is adequate for revealing Him as subsistent existence. The third way therefore appears to be superior to the first and second ways because of the superiority of the effect from which it argues.

Here, too, I would like to note that I do not think I am distorting the Five Ways. In the text cited earlier from the *De Potentia*, Aquinas says:

> For existence is the first and most common effect, and it is more intimate than any other; and therefore such an effect belongs only to God, according to a power proper to Him.[27]

There would seem to be no doubt about Aquinas' view on the relative merits of the various effects from which we argue to first causes; nor would there seem to be any doubt about the correctness of his position. Only existence, or something following on it in the mode of a property, would seem to be proportioned to showing the first cause absolutely.

The difficulty of this third way is considerable. We need only mention the proposition which is most formidable, namely, *omne corruptible aliquando corrumpitur*. As St. Thomas remarks,[28] the argument sustaining it can be considered either logical or metaphysical; but in either case the formality is common and sufficient to conclude about all things whatsoever that are contingent. All who are familiar with the considerations in the *De Caelo* know how inadequately Kant represents the third way when he attacks it.[29]

To conclude my remarks about the third way: once it has been seen to sustain its conclusion, one can then see through the first way that God is the first mover without qualification, and he can see, too, that God is the first agent cause, without qualification, of natural substances. Thus the third way is a fulfillment of the first two ways *according to their own formalities*: absolutely speaking, the first mover and the first agent must be God.

4. *The fourth way.*

The fourth way is probably--at least it seems so to me--the strangest to modern ears. Its argument presupposes a familiarity with a kind of consideration that is foreign to contemporary philosophy. It does, however, argue from that which is common to all things, namely, their transcendental properties together with their existence; it, too, concludes to God under a formality sufficient to establish His existence, and in a way the fourth adds to the third way.

In another presentation of this fourth way--which concludes to something perfect and unparticipated by starting from the imperfect and variously participated--Aquinas remarks:

> One must posit one being [ens] that is most perfectly and truly one being [ens]; and it is proved from the fact that there is a mover that is altogether immobile and most perfect, as is proved by the philosophers. It is necessary therefore that everything less perfect receive existence from the perfect.[30]

Aquinas seems to think that the fourth way presupposes the first, but I would suggest that, when he speaks of the *omnino immobile*, he is saying that the immobile mover is to be taken according to the extended formality.

5. *The fifth way.*

The fifth way presupposes a notion of how goals or ends function as causes, a notion currently not well understood in relation to natural phenomena. It presupposes that a goal is a cause insofar as it is responsible for the determination of an agent antecedent to an action. Everyone knows that goals are first and most properly causes in regard to intelligent agents, but they are also causes in regard to non-intelligent entities insofar as the latter behave regularly in their operations, and insofar as they act on the basis of antecedent determinations responsible for their behavior. Now the fifth way basically says that if an entity is not self-determining, but in fact is determined or oriented toward a determinate end-state or goal, its determination or orientation has been received from another. Now this seems to me to say that the fifth way does not intend to prove the existence of a first cause; instead it shows that the first cause is intelligent. Aquinas remarks: "Ergo est aliquid intelligens . . . ." There is, he says, "something intelligent." He does not argue that something exists, but that something existing is intelligent. However, before one can show that an entity is intelligent, he must have shown that the entity exists. Now, because the kind of goal-direction from which the argument starts is a characteristic of material substances, the effect would be inadequate for concluding to the existence of God as God. On the other hand, the works of physical nature do suffice to show that God is intelligent; for that one does not need a formality which extends to the immaterial realm. If the cause which produces nature is intelligent, so is the cause which is absolutely first, which we know by now to be God.

M. Summary

Our arguments about the order among the proofs depend upon four propositions: (1) no argument can show more in the cause to which it concludes than is contained in the effect; (2) the various effects from which the Five Ways argue are not ontologically equivalent; that is, some effects are realities superior to others; (3) the arguments which start from inferior effects by that fact require other arguments which start from superior effects, which can show more about the first cause. For example, motion, because it is only an instrument in relation to the production of natural substances, requires a principal cause and hence points to an argument concluding to a principal agent of material substance. Similarly, an agent cause of material substances cannot account for superior, immaterial substances under the formality of being an agent responsible for material entities; (4) the human intelligence, because it derives its concepts from sensible entities, knows things according to the inferior formalities before it knows them according to those that are superior. On those grounds we rest our case.

N. Epilogue

Although our principal aim throughout this essay has been to draw attention to certain preliminary and background considerations which are necessary if one is to understand what the proofs are doing, and although no attempt has been made here to discuss the arguments in detail, there remain two issues intrinsic to the proofs upon which I would like to touch for the sake of removing what I consider stumbling blocks to their acceptance. The first of the two issues has an additional aim, which is to illustrate by example one of the considerations omitted from the *Summa* and to show a little of the difficulty that is inherent in the argument. Of course there are many other omissions, also difficult, that cannot be presented here.

The first difficulty has to do with the argument in Book VII of Aristotle's *Physica* which aims at establishing the proposition "Everything that is moved is moved by another."[31] In my judgment, the proof in Book VII is fundamental to the first way and is presupposed to Aristotle's arguments in Book VIII, which, I maintain, would beg the question without the argument of Book VII. Thus my attention will be directed to throwing whatever light I am able on the principal difficulty related to the proposition "Whatever is moved is moved by another."

To begin, the argument in Book VII depends on the notion of mobile entities being continuous and so composed of parts. The first proposition Aristotle lays down says: "Nothing that is moved by itself comes to rest through the coming to rest of anything else that is mobile."[32] On the supposition that there is no need of a mover exterior to the moved, the mobile entity has to be regarded as moving itself, as having a received motion, which Aquinas understands in the following way: "To move itself is nothing other than to be the cause of its own motion. But that which is in some respect cause of itself possesses that of which it is the cause *primo*, for that which is first in some genus is the cause of everything else that is posterior. Hence fire, which is the cause of heat in itself and in other things, is the *primum calidum*."[33]

Now the argument that depends on what is said above is abstract in the sense that it focuses on the *generic* notion of mobile entity as something having magnitude. The argument is a reduction to the impossible and needs no more than the general, abstract notion of the divisibility of the mobile subject *in principle* (not in fact). With that in mind, let us turn to the essential points of the argument.

Aristotle first supposes the mobile to be divided and, on that supposition, if one part stops, the others do too, as a consequence of which the whole is moved through its parts. To assume that the mobile moves itself, however, is to assume that the motion belongs *primo et per se* to the whole and is therefore independent of the parts. Thus, if after the division one part comes to rest and the other continues to move, the whole moves through its parts and not *primo et per se*. In short, the argument claims that, if the motion of the whole depends on the motion of the parts of the mobile subject, the motion must depend on the activity of something extrinsic to the mobile entity; the motion must be received. For the sake of illuminating this proposition, Aquinas, near the end of his commentary, makes the following comparison: just as, if the part were not to exist, the whole would not exist, so too, if the part does not move, then the whole does not move.[34] But, were something to be a *primum mobile* and have its motion from itself, the motion would have to be independent of the parts.

Aquinas provides an analogy to show what this means when he speaks of fire as that which is the *primum calidum*. It must be remembered that in his day fire was considered an elemental substance, and the *calidum* to which reference is made here is not a property but the substance itself, of which the property is simply an index or manifestation. Moreover, if we consider an Aristotelian mixed body, we know that those bodies which were held to be naturally hot were thought to have their natural heat from the fire which composed them. Hence, if such a mixed body were to be divided (physically analyzed) in the proper manner, one would ultimately come to the fire which is cause of the heat in everything else that is natural, including the mixed bodies of which the fire is a composing part. Dividing the substance fire, however, does not result in one part being hot and the other not; on the contrary, no division of the whole yields anything other than two parts, both of which are hot. The reason is that, according to the Aristotelian theory, fire was hot intrinsically in its substance, not merely through a property. So its nature as *primum calidum* was prior to its extension or magnitude and not dependent on it. In short, the *calidum* which is *primum* does not depend on the substance's parts, because it is prior to them, and that is the value of the analogy. The mobile, however, is not the same; for, no matter how far one divides, the mobile as such is continuous and hence dependent on its parts. In sum, there is no possibility of something mobile that is antecedent to magnitude in the way substance is antecedent to magnitude and all its other properties.

With this in mind, we may now make the following point: were some mobile entity to be a *primum mobile* in the sense of the present discussion, it would have to be unextended, which means that motion could not have a physical subject. But that is to deny its character as motion; hence a *primum mobile* in the sense at issue here is impossible.

If my exposition is correct and a *primum mobile* would have to be unextended, why does the Latin commentary speak of motion having to belong to the mobile *primo et per se*, a description which seems to be obscure? The reason, I think, is that "essentially" can be used to signify either that which pertains to the essence of something, or that which, though it is not intrinsic to the essence, follows on it as a necessary property. *Per se* has either of those meanings; so by itself it does not suffice to signify what is at issue in this case. Moreover, *per se* is often used in opposition to *per aliud* and in that case, too, it does not signify that something is intrinsic to the essence. For example, Aquinas says *esse per se convenit formae,* which certainly does not mean that existence is intrinsic to the nature of form; on the contrary, it simply means that existence does not belong to form through another.

In the course of his commentary, Aquinas makes it plain that *per se* is employed in the argument in the sense of *per accidens* and *per partem*, the sense of *per accidens* being extended to include the notion of that which is through a part. But if *primo et per se* is opposed to the notion of being dependent on parts--in this case the parts of a magnitude or extension--then that which is not so dependent would have to pertain to the essence or substance and so be prior in nature to the parts that result from the division of the whole. And, if that were the case, motion would be causal of magnitude and not require the latter as its subject, which is contrary to the very notion of motion. Thus it would seem that,

Preliminaries to the Five Ways 161

because motion requires an extended subject, everything that moves is moved by another; all motion is in some manner received.

The second of the two matters about which I wish to make some comments has to do with the weakness of arguments favoring an infinite series. Apart from the argument in Book VII which is directed against an infinite series of movers on the ground that such a series leads to an infinite motion in a finite time and is therefore impossible, the arguments against an infinite series depend on an inherent weakness which, although in a way obvious, is nonetheless not readily seen; or at least so it seems.

First it ought to be noted that the causes in question should not be thought to be particular causes; that is to say, the infinite series is not to be taken as made up of physical individuals; for example, animal parents. On the contrary, such a series accomplishes nothing; for it fails to take into account something the progenitors cannot cause; namely, the animal's nature as such. If the animal parents were the cause of the animal nature as such, they would be responsible for themselves, since they have the collocation of capacities which constitutes the nature, a state of affairs which is impossible. But now to the root of the difficulty.

As an illustration, consider an electrical device, a bell, say, connected to a battery that supplies a certain amount of current at a certain voltage. Then suppose that although the current is adequate the voltage is not enough to operate the bell and, in order to obtain sufficient voltage, the operator connects another battery in parallel, again measuring the voltage, only to find it still insufficient. He repeats the process, but without ever attaining the necessary voltage. And, if he were to add an infinite number of batteries connected in parallel, he still would not produce the desired effect.

My point, of course, is that arguments which postulate an infinite series are similar to the illustration above, because they postulate causes that in principle cannot account for the effect by themselves, on account of which multiplying them to infinity never overcomes the deficiency inherent in the cause in the first place. That, in my judgment, is why both Aristotle and Aquinas say that an infinite series does not provide a first cause and therefore no mediate cause and therefore no effect. Just as an infinite series of batteries cannot produce a voltage exceeding that of the strongest individual cell, so an infinite series of defective causes cannot overcome the deficiency inherent in each.

College of St. Thomas

St. Paul, Minnesota

NOTES

1. *FR.*

2. I, 11-12; see also St. Thomas' *Commentary*, lectiones 24-29.

3. William L. Rowe, *The Cosmological Argument* (Princeton: Princeton University Press, 1975) 15.

4. The reader ought to see Roy Kenneth Hack, *God in Greek Philosophy* (Princeton: Princeton University Press, 1931). According to Hack, the Greeks almost from the start believed in one God and, by the time Xenophanes had come on the scene, the notion of God had become sophisticated: "We are still in the sixth century B.C., and already Xenophanes has taken the supreme god further along . . . . The One God of Xenophanes has reached the point where substance disappears, and it stands revealed as pure causality and pure unity, unhampered by even the subtlest of physical attributes, except that it "coheres with all that it causes" (p. 61).

5. I would like to stress that the kind of knowledge we have talked about above, imperfect though it may be, has obviously been the foundation for natural religions and their cults.

6. *A Child's Conception of the World*, tr. Joan and Andrew Tomlinson (Totowa, N.J., 1965).

7. Aristotle rightly argues that material causes are the first we come to know in a *systematic way*, a sign of which is that historically the first philosophical-scientific theories were theories of materials.

8. When we say such propositions are "analytically true," we are not using that term in its Kantian or contemporary sense. We mean only that the propositions are recognizably true upon analysis of what the subject and predicate signify, without need of

a middle term, without need of another proposition functioning as a premise from which the necessary connection is inferred. If I say "Certain minerals undergo cleavage because they have weak atomic bonds along a plane," the kind of breaking that is called cleavage--breaking along a smooth plane--is seen to be the necessary consequence of the atomic structure. Given the truth of the premise, the connection between subject and predicate in "Certain (unnamed) minerals undergo cleavage" is seen to be necessary. That, however, is not the way in which the connection between the terms of a *per se notum* proposition is seen.

9. This of course is not to be construed to mean that hypotheses are directly verifiable by observations.

10. Reprinted in *A Writing Apprenticeship*, ed. Norman A. Brittin (New York: Holt, Rinehart and Winston, 1965) 182.

11. *De Partibus Animalium*, ed. W. D. Ross (Oxford: At the Clarendon Press, 1912) 639a 1-12.

12. *Given that the coming-to-be of things is regularly associated with a moving or agent cause*, to assume that either they come to be out of nothing by themselves, or that they exist along with other "universes" in which similar but not identical properties exist (eternally?), is unreasonable. It is irrational to attempt to maintain simultaneously that something comes about regularly in a determinate way and that it need not do so.

13. Let us note here that a variation in an observable always leads us to know that there is some cause even when we do not know precisely what it is. Hypotheses are not required for the former, but they are more often than not required for the latter.

14. We must note that the definition which describes energy physically and not mathematically is commonly given as the *capacity to do work*; and, since work is defined in terms of motion, it is plain that the amount of energy is a measure of the power of an active cause.

15. The question is not, of course, whether something can come to be from nothing as from the absence of a material or materials--which is possible for a creating agent--but from nothing as from the absence of an agent cause, which is impossible.

16. Aristotle and the medievals taught that there were intermediate immaterial causes; separated substances were thought to move the celestial bodies.

17. "Si autem non movetur ab alio in illo genere [motus], sed a se, vel habet virtutem movendi et motum ab alio vel non. Si ab alio, redit argumentum de processu in infinitum; si a se, ergo, sicut habet virtutem, ita et essentiam et esse habet a se, quod est esse improductum et increatum." *Cursus Philosophicus* (Marietti ed.), Vol. II, p. 485.

18. One cannot exaggerate the importance of establishing the existence of substances in nature that are different in kind and that are related as superior to inferior. That issue demands an extensive examination in order to become intelligible to a contemporary philosophical audience. I ask the reader's indulgence when I note that the issue has been considered at some length in a work of mine entitled *Matter and Becoming*, published in 1966 by Priory Press of Chicago. More recently I have finished a more detailed work on the same topic, which is being published under the title *Substance and Modern Science*. It takes into account the data of contemporary science and aims directly at the issue as it is to be understood in such a context. The aim of these remarks is, as I said, to stress the importance of understanding the notion of substance as it applies to natural entities.

19. "In qualibet autem re naturali invenimus quod est ens et quod est res naturalis, et quod est talis vel talis naturae. Quorum *primum* est commune omnibus entibus; *secundum* omnibus res naturalibus; *tertium* in una specie; et *quartum*, si addamus accidentia, est proprium huic individuo." *Q.D. de Potentia*, III, 7c.

20. Of course the question whether a given antecedent, progenitor species is in fact inferior in kind is often difficult to

answer, but that does not affect the argument; for there are *some* inferior and superior species in nature, and that allows the principle to be invoked.

21. If the antecedent agent did nothing more than prepare organic materials, it would be a less proximate cause rather than an active instrument.

22. There is no need to deny it any role at all; on the contrary, it would indeed seem to have a subordinate place.

23. I must add that neither vitalism nor Cartesian dualism is the alternative to mechanism. The issue is discussed in *Substance and Modern Science*.

24. One can say the same for the universal formality of *esse* or existence. The material and the immaterial together constitute an ordered whole that requires one cause. To be the cause of existence as such is to be the cause, not just of species of entities taken as independent classifications, but of the ordered whole the diverse species constitute.

25. By his definitions, the heavy body tended toward the center of the universe, the light body towards its periphery.

26. I might add that current considerations of the anthropic principle can, provided the notion of goal-direction is properly understood, be used to provide an argument to a cause of the fundamental constituents of the universe. A former student of mine, who had no philosophical education beyond logic, after having read George Gale's argument in *Scientific American* on the anthropic principle, said to me, entirely without provocation on my part and somewhat to my surprise, "Why doesn't he [Gale] just come out and say God exists?" The spontaneity of his remark indicates that the mind is contrained to see the conclusion to which the data and the problem point.

27. "Ipsum enim esse est communissimus effectus primus, et intimior omnibus aliis effectibus; et ideo soli Deo competit

secundum virtutem propriam talis effectus . . . ." In another text (*Commentary on St. John's Gospel*, lectio III) he says that every cause other than God acts extrinsically to produce that which is extrinsic to the thing. "Nam alia agentia operantur ut extrinsecus existentia: cum enim non agant nisi movendo et alterando aliquo modo quantum ad ea quae sunt extrinseca rei, ut extrinsecus operantur. Deus vero operatur in omnibus ut interius agens, quia agit in creando. Creare autem est dare esse rei creatae. Cum ergo esse sit intimum cuilibet rei, Deus, qui operando dat esse, operatur in rebus ut intimus agens."

28. Loc. cit.

29. *Critique of Pure Reason*, tr. Norman Kemp Smith (New York: St. Martin's Press, 1965) 507f.

30. "Est autem ponere unum ens, quod est perfectissimum et verissimum ens: quod ex hoc probatur, quia est aliquid movens omnino immobile et perfectissimum, ut a philosophis est probatum. Oportet ergo quod omnia aliia minus perfecta ab ipso esse recipiant." *Q.D. de Potentia*, III, 5.

31. The discussion that follows supposes a familiarity with both Aristotle's text and the commentary of Aquinas.

32. Omne quod movetur a seipso, non quiescit a suo motu per quietem cuiuscumque alterius mobilis.

33. ". . . aliquid movere seipsum nihil aliud est, quam esse sibi causa motus. Quod autem est sibi causa alicuius, oportet quod *primo* ei conveniat; quia quod est primum in quolibet genere, est causa eorum quae sunt post. Unde ignis, qui sibi et aliis est causa caloris, est primum calidum."

34. ". . . haec conditionalis est vera: si pars non movetur, totum non movetur; sicut haec conditionalis est vera: si pars non est, totum non est."

IS "GOD EXISTS" A PROPERLY BASIC BELIEF?

A CONSIDERATION OF ALVIN PLANTINGA'S ARGUMENT

Joseph M. Boyle, Jr.

I. Classical Foundationalism and the Evidentialist Objection to Theism

In "Reason and Belief in God"[1] Professor Alvin Plantinga defends the claim that belief in the existence of God is properly basic for at least some religious persons. In other words, he maintains that at least some theists are altogether reasonable and justified in believing, without evidence, that God exists. He takes a basic proposition to be one that is accepted without evidence from other propositions, and a properly basic proposition to be one that is reasonably taken as basic, a proposition which one is within one's epistemic rights to take as basic.

This claim is introduced to rebut what Plantinga calls "the evidentialist objection" to theistic belief. This objection, made famous by W. K. Clifford and developed by contemporary antitheologians like Michael Scriven and Brand Blanshard, is that religious belief is irresponsible because it goes beyond the evidence for it (24-34). If the belief that God exists is properly basic, then, of course, the evidentialist objection fails. For the objection assumes that this belief is one which should be accepted only on the basis of, and in proportion to the strength of, the relevant evidence. And, if properly basic, belief that God exists is not of that kind, but is such that accepting it without evidence is epistemically proper.

To establish this response Plantinga considers the view he calls "classical foundationalism." This consideration is relevant because the evidentialist objection is usually (but not necessarily) stated in a form which presupposes classical foundationalism (62-63). Classical foundationalism is a species of foundationalism, and foundationalism is a view about rational noetic structures made up of three propositions: "(1) in a rational noetic structure the believed-on-the-basis-of relation is asymmetric and irreflexive; (2) a rational noetic structure has a foundation; and (3) in a rational noetic structure nonbasic belief is proportional in strength to support from the foundations" (55, 61).

Classical foundationalism adds to this generic characterization of foundationalism a set of necessary and sufficient conditions for a belief's being properly basic. Modern classical foundationalists list two such conditions: self-evidence and incorrigibility. Ancient and medieval classical foundationalists do not consider incorrigibility, but add evidence to the senses as a condition. Plantinga puts these three conditions together into what can be called the classical foundationalist conception of proper basicality: "A proposition p is properly basic for a person S if and only if p is either self-evident to S or incorrigible for S or evident to the senses for S" (59).

Plantinga recognizes that classical foundationalism is not the property of evidentialist objectors alone, but is accepted by many Christians as well, particularly by proponents of natural theology, the best known of whom is Aquinas. And so, it seems likely that there is another way to meet the evidentialist objection than by discarding classical foundationalism altogether.

For surely all but the most hardy rationalists among Christians would reject the evidentialist contention that the strength of acceptance of nonbasic belief must be strictly proportioned to the probability of it in relation to properly basic beliefs. Aquinas certainly rejected this contention and held instead that, in the act of faith, there was a certitude not available in human knowledge not moved by grace, and surely not available in other knowledge based on testimony. So, while faith was not held to be basic knowledge, it was held to be more certain than the evidence for it.[2] More generally, there often seem to be good reasons for accepting a nonbasic proposition more strongly than the evidence warrants, provided there is some evidence for it.

That, at least, is what the proponent of natural theology is likely to hold and, while the line of reasoning needs development, it does provide a different line of response to the evidentialist objector than the one Plantinga favors. But Plantinga seems to cut off this approach by including in the definition of foundationalism the requirement that the strength of acceptance of nonbasic beliefs must, in a rational noetic structure, be proportioned to their probability in relation to properly basic beliefs. So perhaps foundationalism should not be understood as including this proportionality thesis. If it is, then natural theologians like Aquinas should not be considered foundationalists, even though they hold part of what foundationalists hold, accepting the classical foundationalist conception of proper basicality.

This conception is what Plantinga objects to, but it is worth noting that it can be accepted by those who agree with Plantinga that evidentialism is mistaken. It seems, therefore, that Plantinga's dissatisfaction with classical foundationalism is based not simply on his concern that it provides, perhaps unwittingly, support to evidentialism.

II. Does Plantinga Establish the Collapse of Classical Foundationalism?

Plantinga establishes his central conclusion, that "God exists" is a properly basic belief, by refuting classical foundationalism, and then by answering objections to his own, "Reformed" conception of basic knowledge. His refutation of classical foundationalism has two components: an argument that it is false and a distinct argument that it is self-referentially inconsistent. In this section I will spell out his arguments for these claims and criticize them.

A. Plantinga's Arguments that Classical Foundationalism is False

His argument that classical foundationalism is false has two parts. The first is that classical foundationalism leads to the absurd conclusion that enormous quantities of what we all believe are irrational to believe. One of the lessons of modern philosophy is that, relative to what is self-evident and incorrigible, most of our everyday beliefs are not probable, or at least not shown to be such. For example, all the propositions which entail that there are enduring physical bodies, and persons other than oneself, and that the past is real, are more probable than not with respect to what is self-evident or incorrigible. If we add to the foundations propositions evident to the senses, then propositions entailing the existence of material objects are added to the foundations, but that addition does not show how propositions about other selves, or about the past, can be probable (59-60).

The second part of his argument that classical foundationalism is false is that many beliefs which do not meet the conditions for proper basicality of classical foundationalism are properly basic, for example, Plantinga's belief on the day he wrote his piece that he had lunch at noon. Plantinga maintains that this proposition is basic for him; he believes it on the basis of no other proposition, and he is entirely rational in doing so. He recognizes that the foundationalist can object--either that it is basic for Plantinga but improperly so, or that it is not in fact taken as basic (60).

Before criticizing these arguments, I should note that I will consider Plantinga's criticisms only as they apply to ancient and medieval foundationalism, that is, to that form of classical foundationalism according to which a proposition is properly basic if and only if it is either self-evident or evident to the senses. If incorrigibility is a distinct condition for proper basicality, as modern foundationalists seem to have thought, then I am simply defending less than they. But incorrigibility is often thought of as a condition for any other condition for proper basicality--that what is self-evident must also be incorrigible, or that what is experientially evident must also be incorrigible. This I reject. Further, on the premodern conception of scientific knowledge, not only self-evident principles but also demonstrated conclusions are certain.

Modern foundationalists surely must feel the force of Plantinga's first argument. For their notion of self-evidence allows few propositions to be taken as self-evident, and there is little beyond introspective reports which could be incorrigible. Relative to such narrow foundations, very little of what people think about themselves and the world around them can be shown to be probable. But does the development of modern philosophy have lessons for premodern foundationalists as well?

Premodern classical foundationalists had rather different preoccupations than modern philosophers. In particular, their concerns about epistemology were largely limited to the epistemology of science. Questions of faith and reason were, of course, central to medieval reflection, but, these aside, there was relatively little thought about the epistemology of everyday, common sense knowledge, such as the knowledge of contingent, empirical facts. Thinkers like Aquinas appear to have thought that people's beliefs about such matters could be rationally justified. But they did not provide a full account of how they distinguished within these beliefs between those that are immediately known and those known by evidence from more basic beliefs; nor did they elaborate an explanation of the evidencing relationship between such beliefs. But the existence of these lacunae does not show that premodern foundationalism lacks the resources to deal with such questions.

Moreover, the lessons of modern philosophy seem largely irrelevant to our estimate of the prospects for such a development. For the premodern foundationalists operated with a far richer notion of self-evidence than modern philosophers: a proposition was held to be self-evident if the intelligibility of the predicate term in a proposition was immediately connected with or contained in the subject term. Thus, "All men are rational animals" is taken by Aquinas as a typical example of a proposition known through itself--*per se notum*. Propositions known through themselves are not, as Plantinga's examples tend to suggest, limited to truths of logic or analytic truths. Further, propositions evident to the senses, however the precise boundaries of this category are to be understood, are not limited to Chisholmian reports of experience such as "I am appeared to redly."

These differences are relevant to the examples Plantinga uses. As he, in effect, admits, Aquinas appears to have held that the reality of the material world was evident to the senses: that is, he held that propositions about the external world could be known to be true, and this knowledge entails the reality of the external world.

Of course, this belief in the reality of the external world is subject to skeptical challenge on the basis of philosophical arguments like those often mounted by modern philosophers. Premodern foundationalists can meet this challenge on its own philosophical terms, but unless this challenge is successful--not only against philosophers like Descartes and Locke but against earlier foundationalits like Aquinas and Aristotle--then the belief in the external world, based on sense experience, is not put in doubt.

Why not say the same kind of thing with respect to the other common sense propositions Plantinga considers? On the basis of sense experience, including memory, we make judgments about the past, including such judgments as "something moves," which is evident to the senses and which entails the reality of at least the very recent past.

Of course, skeptical arguments can be mounted to show that all memory is illusory. Responding to those arguments, however, is dialectic which does not replace the basic knowledge of the past which is evident in sense experience. Plantinga recognizes that

Is "God Exists" A Basic Belief? 175

such argumentation can be important for the rational accepance of basic knowledge, but does not render such knowledge nonbasic (82-84).

The case of other minds is perhaps more interesting because our beliefs about other minds do not, on the classical foundationalist conception of proper basicality, seem to be properly basic. That there are other persons does not seem self-evident, nor is it evident to the senses. For we cannot have sensory awareness of the minds of other persons. But we can observe their behaviour, including their talk, and note that some of it is unique to human beings, and infer that the behaviour must be the activity of beings having capacities similar to our own. Let us suppose that this is how we come to know other persons.

This gives us a case where the lessons of modern philosophy should apply. For we have nonbasic knowledge which is held to be somehow probable in relation to the relevant basic propositions. Clearly, there is controversy about the inference from what is evident to the senses to the nonbasic belief in other minds. No doubt, philosophers who accept only incorrigible or narrowly self-evident propositions will find this inference unwarranted, but others with a more ample conception of the foundations will hardly be impressed by this. Still, even these latter will make use of some causal principle which seems neither evident to the senses nor self-evident, some such principle as that the activity of something must be grounded in the capacity of the thing to perform that activity. Some premodern classical foundationalists would no doubt hold that this principle is either self-evident or entailed by what is self-evident. Suppose, however, that it is not self-evident nor derivable from what is. Does this render the inference based upon it not probable with respect to what is basic? I think not. For, to the extent that this assumption is reasonable, inferences based on it are probable in the relevant sense, and their conclusions are, clearly, given evidence by the properly basic propositions.

In short, a nod in the direction of the lessons of modern philosophy, and a reminder that no one has shown how many everyday beliefs are justified by the foundations, are not sufficient to show that premodern foundationalism is false. These considerations show only that this version of foundationalism is incompletely developed.

But Plantinga has another argument that classical foundationalism is false--namely, that some beliefs which would not be properly basic by this account clearly are properly basic. His example is his belief that he had lunch at noon, but he also regards belief in other minds to be of this kind (81-82).

Such beliefs as these may appear to be basic because one usually accepts them without any explicit awareness of other propositions on whose evidence they are believed. One is not aware of making inferences from other propositions. But this is hardly a sure sign that a proposition is basic, let alone properly so. For, even when one does not consider evidence for a belief, one may well have that evidence, as it were, in the back of one's mind. One may simply take it for granted that another person exists until questioned, and then, more or less immediately, give evidence for one's belief. So it does not follow from the fact that we usually do not stop and make inferences from people's behaviour to their reality as persons that belief in this reality is basic. So it seems too strong a condition for basicality that one has no evidence explicitly in mind.

This consideration is relevant to appraising Plantinga's view that a fourteen-year-old Christian, brought up in a community of believers, can believe, with no evidence whatsoever, that God exists. He has never heard of the arguments of natural theology, and does not believe on the basis of the testimony of his fellows. Surely, Plantinga is focusing on the fact that the young Christian does not go through a process of reasoning when he accepts propositions entailing God's existence. But if asked he might well appeal to rudimentary versions of natural theological arguments or to the testimony of people he trusts; and perhaps, if he did not, that might be because of a lack of ability to articulate what at some level he understood.

Turning to his example about lunch at noon, there is no reason to think that some beliefs based on memory cannot be evident to the senses. If something so far distant as noontime cannot be based simply on memory, then perhaps it is not properly basic. In this case other propositions, not just one's experience of remembering, would be evidence for the belief. One need not explicitly consider these propositions--for example, that one always has lunch at noon or that one is not now hungry as one would be if lunch were skipped--but they would be evidence, which one might easily recite if asked for reasons why one accepted such a belief. Then again, maybe the belief was properly basic, and the relevant experience included not only one's memory but one's present awareness of satiety.

B. The Argument that Classical Foundationalism Is Self-Referentially Inconsistent

But all this seems to be by way of preliminary skirmishing. The argument that classical foundationalism is self-referentially inconsistent is introduced as perhaps more convincing. The argument is straightforward: "Classical foundationalism must be rationally acceptable by its own standards of rationality. Thus, its criterion for proper basicality must be either a properly basic proposition or a proposition properly grounded upon basic propositions. But classical foundationalism does not itself meet its criterion. For it is neither a self-evident proposition nor a proposition evident to the senses, nor is there any argument for it based upon either of the above. Thus, the statement of the classical foundationalist criterion is either false (falsified, as it were, by its own acceptance) or such that in accepting it the classical foundationalist is violating his epistemic responsibilities (if assumed true, it would be the kind of proposition whose acceptance is outlawed by the standard it sets)." Plantinga rightly concludes that one ought not to believe a proposition which is true only if one ought not to believe it (60-62).

All this, Plantinga recognizes, depends on there not being an argument from properly basic propositions to the foundationalist criterion of proper basicality. For, if there is such an argument, there is no need to take the statement of the criterion as either evident to the senses or self-evident.

And there does seem to be more of an argument than Plantinga recognizes. The idea is as follows. The business of knowing and believing has a purpose--the achievement of cognitive states that are true. Thus, propositions should be believed only if there is reason to think them true.

Nonbasic propositions can be known to be true only by determining how they are evidenced by other propositions it is reasonable to think true. At some point, there must be propositions it is reasonable to think true independently of the truth of other propositions. As Plantinga notes, no one has time to continually consider infinitely many propositions as evidence for a given belief. So some propositions must be basic.

But, to do their job, basic propositions must be true, or must at least be such that accepting them presumptively puts one in touch with reality. Thus, although as basic they do not need evidence from other propositions, they nevertheless must be evident. Let us call the evidence of basic propositions "immediate evidence." This feature is what makes properly basic propositions able to function as the foundation of a rational noetic structure.

This discussion suggests a proposition which seems to be self-evident: that properly basic propositions must be immediately evident. The immediacy is required by the basicality of the proposition; the evidence by the exigency of functioning properly with regard to cognitive states that are true and known to be such.

No doubt it is unfashionable to hold that human minds can be united with reality in the way demanded by this proposition. But here it is not the unfashionable proposition, but rather its denial, which is in danger of self-referential inconsistency. Do we know just enough about the limits of human knowledge to know that no proposition can be evident in this sense? Or are we sufficiently united to the way things are to know only that this is the only proposition that is properly basic in the sense required?

Plantinga accepts the idea that self-evidence and evidence to the senses are sufficient for proper basicality (59). Why is that? Because "evidence" in these expressions refers to a self-conscious union between the knower and reality? Plantinga maintains that even properly basic beliefs are not groundless. They have circumstances which confer justification, and in the case of perceptual judgments these circumstances include having the appropriate sensations, which contribute both to forming the belief and to justifying it (79).

But it is not clear from what Plantinga says that justification means giving evidence in the sense I have been suggesting. For he seems to reserve the term "evidence" to the relation between propositions. And, while it seems reasonable to understand justification as giving immediate evidence in the case of perceptual judgments, both his general definition of a justified belief and his discussion of the grounds which justify taking "God exists" as properly basic suggest otherwise.

He calls a belief justified for a person at a given time if the person is violating no epistemic duties and is within his epistemic rights in accepting it then, and if the person's noetic structure is not defective in virtue of his accepting it (79). This definition appears to include the justification of nonbasic propositions, and, more importantly, to allow as proper basic propositions propositions which are not immediately evident. For the conditions which justify taking "God exists," or more precisely other propositions which entail this one, as justified basic beliefs, are not conditions which make these propositions immediately evident. Rather they seem to be conditions which trigger, or call forth, the theological beliefs in question (80-81). Belief in God, Plantinga appears to follow Calvin in maintaining, is something we have an ineradicable tendency or disposition to accept under certain conditions (80). And the disposition to believe something is not evidence for it.

So Plantinga might wish to deny the unfashionable proposition which is at the heart of classical foundationalism. But this proposition does not seem self-referentially inconsistent or false and, even if it is not self-evident, as I believe it to be, it is surely a proposition there is good reason to accept. Insisting that the foundations of belief should correspond to reality is surely not an eccentric view.

Still, this proposition is not the only controversial part of the classical foundationalist view. What is contested, even if this unfashionable proposition is allowed, is the narrow meaning given to "immediately evident" by classical foundationalists. Why should only self-evident propositions and those evident to the senses be allowed as immediately evident?

The classical account begins with the division of immediately evident propositions into those that are evident of themselves and those that are evident in virtue of something beyond themselves. The division seems complete. The first category is that of self-evident propositions, but what outside the proposition itself could count as immediate, nonpropositional evidence for a proposition?

Sense experience is an obvious candidate, but is there anything else? Perhaps the activity of the mind in understanding and judging sense experience provides a distinct source of immediate evidence for some propositions. Aquinas may have thought this, but he held that knowledge of the activity of the mind was not primary, that it presupposed sensory experience which provided the object for human knowledge.[3]

Aquinas thought that he had established that all propositional knowledge depended, more or less directly, upon sense experience. The claim was not that humans could form propositions about sense experience only, or that the truth of every proposition could be establishd only in sense experience, but that the concepts out of which propositions are constructed were abstracted from sense experience. Thus, for Aquinas, there is nothing which could provide immediate evidence for propositions except the sensory experience from which the propositions emerged, and perhaps the intellect's immediate awareness of its activity of understanding and judging. Other sources of immediate evidence are not to be found, and so any knowledge which is not included in these sources must be inferential and derivative.[4]

No doubt Plantinga would want to reject this Thomistic account of the origins of knowledge, but doing this would require close examination of a set of complex arguments about human nature and the nature of knowing. Moreover, Aquinas went to some lengths to show how his view of human knowldge could account for scientific, mathematical, and metaphysical knowledge.[5] So, it is unlikely that there are obvious counterexamples to Aquinas' view.

The point, however, is that, to subvert the classical foundationalist conception of proper basicality, it is necessary to overturn arguments like Aquinas' on the nature of human knowledge, or to show that the underlying conviction that properly basic propositions must be immediately evident is indefensible. Plantinga has done neither.

Further, if the underlying conviction is allowed to stand, the Thomistic account of human knowledge contains a challenge to one who accepts as properly basic propositions which are neither evident to the senses nor self-evident: if there is some other way in which propositions can be immediately evident, then what is it? Where in human experience is the factor which would make such a proposition evident?

III. Does Plantinga Show that Belief in God is Properly Basic?

Plantinga thinks, of course, that rejecting classical foundationalism removes the main stumbling block to considering the belief in God as properly basic. For, if the classical foundationalist conception of proper basicality is defensible, the necessary conditions for proper basicality which belief in God does not meet can themselves be set aside. But showing that the standard reasons for denying that belief in God is properly basic are not sound does not by itself establish that this belief is properly basic. As my questions of the preceding paragraph suggest, the claim that belief in God is properly basic is establishd only if one shows that it meets some condition sufficient for proper basicality. Plantinga has not shown this.

He recognizes that he needs further argumentation to make it plausible, even after the rejection of classical foundationalism, that belief in God is properly basic. But these arguments do not show what it is about the Christian's belief in God which renders that belief properly basic.

One important part of that argumentation is Plantinga's elaboration of his view about how to arrive at conditions for proper basicality. His view is that there are such conditions, and consequently the Reformed epistemologist is not committed to holding that just any outlandish belief might qualify as properly basic.

He draws an analogy between those who reject classical foundationalism and those who reject the verifiability criterion of meaning. These latter are not, by their rejection of positivism, committed to saying that one can rule out no sentence whatsoever as meaningless. Even if unequipped with a general criterion of meaning, one who encounters, let us say, a nonsense verse can rightly reject it as meaningless, and by reflecting on this rejection articulate the relevant conditions. So also the Reformed epistemologist who rejects classical foundationalism is not thereby committed to allowing any belief as properly basic. Belief that the Great Pumpkin comes every Halloween might be basic for some people, but the Reformed epistemologist is not required to allow it as proper (74-75).

So, it is possible on Plantinga's account to arrive at conditions for proper basicality, but they must be arrived at inductively, by considering examples like the Great Pumpkin and developing conditions which fit the cases. This particularist approach to developing conditions for proper basicality might or might not lead to a general criterion for proper basicality, but it can establish some necessary and some sufficient conditions for proper basicality (75-77).

Plantinga recognizes that there is likely to be disagreement about examples. He insists, however, that the examples to which the Christian community is bound are its own, not the examples of antitheists (77).

Even remaining with examples acceptable to the Christian community--examples, presumably, of beliefs that are obviously properly basic, and of some that are obviously not, and of some that are not obviously either--Plantinga gives no reason for thinking that belief in God is properly basic. He surely gives no reason for thinking that it is immediately evident, and does not argue that such a belief can be properly basic even though it is not immediately evident. What we have is only the conviction of the Christian community that belief in God is properly basic. And the only considerations in favor of that conviction are the fact that members of the Christian community all have an irrepressible tendency to accept the belief in certain circumstances, that they do not have evidence in mind when they accept this belief, and perhaps that they are aware of the belief as unshakably certain. If these things make a belief properly basic, are we not entitled to some account of how and why?

To sum up: Plantinga has not shown that belief in God is properly basic. His arguments against the classical foundationalist conception of proper basicality do not clearly address, much less refute, the underlying conviction of that view--that properly basic beliefs must be immediately evident. Further, he does not dispute on its own terms the reasoning for limiting immediately evident propositions to those that are self-evident or evident to the senses. He proposes a broader conception of proper basicality, but gives neither reasons why beliefs neither self-evident nor evident to the senses should be thought immediately evident, nor convincing reasons why we should suppose there are properly basic beliefs which are not immediately evident.

St. Michael's College

University of Toronto

NOTES

1. *FR*, 18-93. All further references to this article will be made in the text to the relevant pages.

2. See *Scriptum Super Librum III Sententiarum*, Distinctio XXIII, Quaestio II, Quaestiuncula 3, Solutio 2. For a fuller discussion of this and related texts and their relevance to Plantinga's argument, see Joseph M. Boyle Jr., J. Hubbard, and Thomas D. Sullivan, "The Reformed Objection to Natural Theology: A Catholic Perspective," *Christian Scholars Review*, 9 (1982) 206-211.

3. *Summa Theologiae*, Prima Pars, 87, 3.

4. *Summa Theologiae*, Prima Pars, 84, 3-7; 85, 1; Qq. 87-88.

5. See *In Librum Boetii de Trinitate*, Quaestiones 5-6; for an accessible English Translation, see Armand Maurer, translator, *The Division and Methods of the Sciences* (Toronto: The Pontifical Institute of Medieval Studies, 1963).

"REFORMED" EPISTEMOLOGY

Thomas A. Russman, O.F.M. Cap.

Perhaps there is a trap in giving a project the title "Toward a Reformed View of Faith and Reason."[1] Such a title appears to assume that there *is* a *Reformed* view of such matters that is different enough from other views to warrant separate classification. If the participants in the project assume this, they may be inclined to exaggerate differences with other views in order to vindicate this assumption--to give their new bird called "Reformed epistemology" its own preening branch to stand on, as it were. Whether it was such inclinations that actually caused the sorts of confusions one sometimes finds in *Faith and Rationality*, I am in no position to say; but the confusions are the sort one *might well expect if one thought* that such inclinations held sway.

The *raison d'être* of any project whose title carries the adjectives "Reformed" or "Protestant" is that which is to be "reformed" or "protested against." In a theological context, what was historically to be reformed or protested against was "Catholic Christianity," to speak broadly, or "Medieval Christianity," to speak more narrowly. To take an epistemological stand against these is presumably to stand with the "moderns," to stand fundamentally with the philosophies which arose from the 16th century onward.

Now, the participants in this contemporary Reformed project do not embrace modernity without qualification. They are

"Christian," after all, and not just "Reformed." As a fellow Christian I hold it immensely to their credit that when there seems to be a conflict between their need to stake out unique "Reformed" territory and their commitment to be Christian first and above all--they all finally side with the latter. I say *finally* they so side--there are times on first reading when the issue might appear to be in doubt.

Reformed Christians cannot embrace modern, post-16th-century epistemologies without qualification, because these epistemologies tend to be incompatible with Christian Faith. Plantinga and Wolterstorff develop a critique of modern epistemologies that embody what they call "classical foundationalism" and commit what they call "the evidentialist fallacy." But how then shall "*Reformed* epistemology" be *modern* in the way its name would seem to require? Wolterstorff sees it as a "contribution to the general, postfoundationalist dialogue on epistemology that is now taking place."[2] When this way of locating Reformed epistemology in the modern era is coupled with Plantinga's attempt to classify Thomas Aquinas as a "classical foundationalist" guilty of the "evidentialist fallacy," the outcome could not seem more jolly for the Reformed project. The aspects of modern epistemology to be avoided are just the ones that perpetuate variations of earlier mistakes found in Thomas Aquinas, taken as the high expression of Catholic, medieval Christianity. Reformed epistemology, by contrast, is as modern and up to date as you please, contributing to the "postfoundationalist dialogue on epistemology that is now taking place," a dialogue premised on the rejection of precisely those earlier aberrations. The apparent neatness of this Reformed view stands, I believe, upon a three-legged confusion about the postfoundationalist dialogue, about Thomas Aquinas, and about how both relate to the Reformed epistemology presented.

A. The Postfoundationalist Dialogue

Wolterstorff's enthusiasm for the contemporary, postfoundationalist dialogue in epistemology is precisely the point which might at first seem to put his Christianity in doubt. He immediately distances himself from the views of such prominent postfoundationalists as Richard Rorty and Paul Feyerabend.[3] These postfoundationalists are said to be "agnostic" and "antinomian," which Reformed epistemology, we are told, is not. But the characteristic tenet of mainstream postfoundationalist thought (that of Wittgenstein, Sellars, Quine, Putnam, Kuhn, and many others--not just of Feyerabend and Rorty) is that there can be *no* foundations for knowledge. Postfoundationalism has, in other words, implied antifoundationalism. If one is going to be *post*foundationalist, one is not going to be foundationalist at all.

Now, the thought of our Reformed brethren declaring for antifoundationalism would have a most saddening effect upon many of their less Reformed fellow Christians. Let's state the matter categorically--Christianity is epistemologically a foundationalist enterprise. It claims that revelation has taken place, that, whatever developments in Christian understanding may emerge, the validity of those developments is always to be checked against the foundation in revelation. Indeed, the Reformers themselves claimed that the Church had become unfaithful to its foundations. They championed a return to the foundational roots they characteristically conceived narrowly as *sola scriptura*. The objective had been, after all, *reform* of *Christianity*--not the establishment of a new religion on new foundations. And so, if some of our Reformed brothers and sisters were at this late hour to embrace antifoundationalism, they would be abandoning some of the most central and most commonly held tenets concerning Christian revelation. The grounds on which they might continue to call themselves "Christian" would not be the grounds on which *Christians* have called themselves Christian through the centuries to the present.

It turns out, however, and to our relief, that Wolterstorff, Plantinga, and Company are not antifoundationalists. Indeed, as we shall see, a more foundationalist group of thinkers one could hardly expect to find. Then why their flirtation with this self-image of being in the center of recent epistemological trends, given the antifoundationalist nature of these trends? A primary target of the antifoundationalist vogue has been what Wolterstorff and Plantinga call "classical" foundationalism. (This name is an anachronism, I shall argue later.) Since they too would target "classical" foundationalism, they insouciantly act as though this entitles them to membership in the postfoundationalist club. Indeed, they appear to enjoy dressing themselves up as full-fledged antifoundationalists. Even though they make it clear that the only sort of foundationalism they mean to attack is "classical" foundationalism, they frequently drop the word "classical" and simply speak as though "foundationalism" taken as a whole were to be rejected. Now, the latter is exactly what true postfoundationalists say, but it is not what Plantinga or Wolterstorff can or do say. They confuse the issue greatly when they neglect to make the distinction, even offering main headings with such titles as "The Collapse of Foundationalism," when it is clear that the collapse of only "classical" foundationalism is meant.

When we examine Reformed epistemology as presented by Plantinga and Wolterstorff, the incongruity of its purported association with the postfoundationalist mainstream becomes evident. In what ways does this Reformed epistemology differ from "classical" foundationalism? It simply adds further foundations to the ones considered acceptable to "classical" foundationalists. To the list of basic propositions--which for the "classical" foundationalist includes only propositions which are self-evident or which are about one's own states of consciousness or which are evident to the senses--the Reformed epistemologist would add propositions such as "God exists" and "God has forgiven my sins." How can anyone familiar with the postfoundationalist mainstream think that its drift is to *add further strong* foundations to those held by "classical" foundationalism? Rather, its drift is to declare all purported foundations "framework relative": the so-called "foundations" merely express question-begging adherence to a language game that is in principle dispensable. Reformed epistemology and the postfoundationalist mainstream would appear to be moving in exactly opposite directions--one appealing to a greatly increased store of dependable basic propositions, the other undermining even the smaller store of such propositions accepted by "classical" foundationalism. The common repudiation of "classical" foundationalim should not be allowed to obscure this rather complete difference between Reformed epistemology as presented by Plantinga and Wolterstorff and mainstream postfoundationalist epistemology.

B. Thomas Aquinas

Alvin Plantinga tells us that Thomas Aquinas is a "classical" foundationalist. Let's see what this means. A foundationalist holds that all knowledge is or is based upon a privileged sort of knowledge, which is the foundation of *all other* knowledge. A "*classical*" foundationalist is one who limits the range of foundational knowledge to a few characteristic types and who insists that all other knowledge must be derivable from this foundational knowledge by strictly logical operations. Plantinga tells us that the *modern* "classical" foundationalist limits the range of foundational or basic propositions to those that are self-evident or that are about introspectible states (and therefore incorrigible). The ancient or medieval "classical" foundationalist adds to these two types of basic propositions a third type: propositions that are evident to the senses. Thomas Aquinas is, according to Plantinga, a medieval "classical" foundationalist.

Plantinga's interpretation of Aquinas is curiously maladroit. Even the texts which he quotes should have led him to a very different interpretation. He attributes to Aquinas a distinction between "knowledge" and "faith": "[T]he vast majority of those who believe in God, he [Aquinas] thinks, do not have knowledge of God's existence but must instead take it on faith."[4] Plantinga goes on to emphasize twice more that, for Aquinas, such "taking on faith" is not "*knowledge*," the latter being possible only through *demonstrations* of God's existence. Now, this way of distinguishing between faith and knowledge is clearly *not* Aquinas' view, as is manifest from the very texts Plantinga cites in support of it. Aquinas makes it clear that he regards faith as a source of *knowldge*, and he explicitly denies that "strict demonstration" is "the only way to reach a knowledge of the things we must know about God."[5]

Why does Aquinas say that Faith gives knowledge? Because Christian Faith is belief that what God has revealed is true--there could be no more reliable source of information. But how does one know that it is God who is doing the revealing? Plantinga once again cites an appropriate text in which Aquinas clearly takes himself to be offering evidence for divine revelation. Aquinas mentions the miracles that accompanied the proclamation of the Gospel, the wonderfully good effects it produced in those who accepted it, the testimony of sacrifice on the part of those who preached it, the extraordinary goodness and brilliance of the doctrine itself, and so on. Plantinga is right to say that Aquinas offers such considerations as *evidence* for divine revelation; he is also right, in my opinion, to attribute to Aquinas the view that *some* such evidence is needed for one reasonably to accept a revelation as coming from God. But it does not follow from these two points, as Plantinga thinks it does, that Aquinas is a "classical" foundationalist. To fall into *this* category Aquinas would also have to hold that the relationship between evidence and conclusion here is one of "strict demonstration." In the text already cited Aquinas denies that such demonstration is needed for knowledge. The emphasis he places upon the essential role of the Holy Spirit in enabling people to recognize the hand of God in the various types of evidence shows that, in his view, the process is not one of strict rational demonstration--for the latter requires no such activity of the Holy Spirit. For Aquinas there is a logically irreducible component in the process of going from the relevant evidence to the acknowledgment that *God* is at work revealing. Let's call this logically irreducible component "insight."

A properly disposed individual, illuminated by the Holy Spirit, while considering relevant evidence, is able to acknowledge by insight the working and presence of God. The movement from consideration of evidence to acknowledgment of God is not demonstration. Nor does Aquinas speak of it as the amassing of probabilities as did such 19th century apologists as Paley and Butler. Plantinga unfairly projects these later "probability" views upon Aquinas.[6] For Aquinas one arrives at the firmest knowledge, not at anything that could be adequately described as "very highly probable."

From the insight "God is at work" or "God is speaking," it does follow that God exists. The knowledge of God's existence is not separated from the recognitiion of God acting. For Aquinas, human knowledge that something exists is always connected with specific manifestations of that existence--questions of existence cannot be treated in isolation from the evidence of such manifestations, or from the recognition of such manifestations for what they are.

Plantinga's failure to understand the role of what I have called "insight" in Aquinas' position explains his mystification at what he calls "another line of thought in Aquinas." Plantinga cites a text in which Aquinas acknowledges that one can arrive at *natural* knowledge of God without strict demonstration: "For, when men see that things in nature run according to a definite order, and that ordering does not occur without an orderer, they perceive in most cases that there is some orderer of the things that they see."[7] Plantinga believes this text to be at variance with Aquinas' general doctrine, because the process it describes does not fit "classical" foundationalism--the latter being, in his view, what Aquinas holds. Plantinga suggests that "perhaps here we must see Aquinas as an early Calvinist."[8] This last remark, whether ingenuous or disingenuous, is certainly hilarious--as if all the countless Christian thinkers before Calvin who held something like this position were but anticipations!

Once we understand the role of what I have called "insight" in going from evidence to conclusions, we have no difficulty understanding this last text as just a further application of Aquinas' general doctrine, here to the exercise of natural intelligence (i.e., intelligence unaided by supernatural assistance such as that from the Holy Spirit). The evidence, in this case, is the order of the universe and the fact that intelligence and power can be used to produce order. From this evidence it is possible to move, by a process including insight, to the recognition of an orderer of stupendous intelligence and power. This last is "the confused knowledge of God which is found in practically all men."

Plantinga's failure to understand Aquinas is never greater than on the issue of memory. After calling Aquinas a "classical" foundationalist, he says that matters of memory cannot be basic for the "classical" foundationalist.[9] But it is patently false to say that Aquinas does not accept remembered facts (such as that I had breakfast this morning) as foundational. This is just not a skepticism Aquinas has any tendency toward. Once again, it would appear, Plantinga is projecting back upon Aquinas aberrations that are easily found in later writers.

C. Aristotle

At one point in Plantinga's discussion, when a text from Aquinas puzzles him, he remarks that it is hard to fit that text into Aquinas' "Aristotelian way of looking at the matter."[10] From this I take it that Plantinga thinks Aristotelians in general and Aristotle in particular are "classical" foundationalists. Was it this preconception that disposed Plantinga to force this interpretation upon Aquinas? Is Aristotle a "classical" foundationalist?

Aristotle's *Posterior Analytics* appears to describe scientific knowledge in the "classical" foundationalist mode, as a structure with only necessary and essential premises at its base and all other knowledge derivable from this base via syllogisms. If our understanding of Aristotle's view of scientific knowledge came only from reading the *Posterior Analytics*, we would seem justified in declaring him a "classical" foundationalist.

But Aristotle *employed* scientific method, he did not merely *talk about* it. And when Aristotle is pursuing science in his *Metaphysics*, in his *De Anima*, or in his works of natural science, he does not adhere to the requirements laid down in the *Posterior Analytics*. Many of his moves require that syllogism be supplemented by insight. I have heard William Wallace argue that Aristotle's method in the *Physics* is very close to that described in the *Posterior Analytics*. But, to my knowledge, neither Wallace nor anyone has argued that Aristotle's other works exhibit the pure method of the *Posterior Analytics*. Assuming that these other works do not, what are we to conclude about the resulting discrepancy between Aristotelian method *in theory* and Aristotelan method *in practice*. Which one shows us the true Aristotle?

The answer to this question depends, I think, upon one's general view of the Aristotelian enterprise. Historically there has always been tension between the study of logic, of the formal connections between propositions, and the study of how people actually arrive at knowledge. Many philosophers have concentrated on logic and have ruled out any "so-called knowledge" that does not adhere to the canons of logic. The result is the philosophy of the methodologists; it generally leads to a high degree of skepticism as it is discovered that not much that humans have taken to be knowledge can pass the logician's test. Plato the logician could not understand how knowledge of necessary truths could be derived from the observation of contingent things. He concluded that it cannot be, and that all knowledge is derived from innate contact with some logically pure realm of eternal forms. Aristotle balked at this logician's paradise. He made the study of how people actually come to know primary to his own epistemology. It was obvious to him that people do derive knowledge of necessary truths from observation. He took this as given and set out to explain it. Furthermore, he did not let the logician's objections to induction blind him to the fact that, carefully done, inductive moves could be brilliantly successful. He pursued the truth any way he could get it, rather than by limping along bereft of proven methods just because the latter lacked pure logical justification. In doing this Aristotle sided with "insight" as an important component of the proper use of evidence. In fact, insight functions extensively in Aristotle's pursuit of scientific knowledge. For this he makes no apology. Whether he recognized it at the time he wrote the *Posterior Analytics* or not, Aristotle came to see that the method described there was not a complete description of all the power available to the human knower. If I am right in this interpretation, and I find the general evidence very convincing, Aristotle himself is not a "classical" foundationalist; and Aquinas can be seen as most Aristotelian when he shows how evidence may be used to arrive at conclusions in ways not justifiable by the canons of logic alone.

What this would also show is that so-called "classical" foundationalism is almost entirely a modern affair. Aristotle's epistemology does not fit it because of the implicit role of insight in his methodology. Plato's epistemology does not fit it because of the extremely broad base of virtually mystical intuitions he allows. Who then would be the "classical" foundationalists before the 16th century? Since "classical" is a word ordinarily used to denote the ancient Greek and Roman period, it is very misleading to use it to designate an almost entirely modern phenomenon. I suggest that we drop the word "classical" and substitute another word, like "formal" or "logical." The likes of Bacon, Russell, Carnap, and Wittgenstein are the culprits we have in mind--not Plato, Aristotle, Augustine, or Aquinas.

D. The Reformers

Since Plantinga is not too shy to tell us about Aquinas, I shall match his temerity and venture some remarks about John Calvin. Plantinga tells us, "What the Reformers meant to hold is that it is entirely right, rational, reasonable, and proper to believe in God *without any evidence* or argument at all; in this respect belief in God resembles belief in the past, in the existence of other persons, and in the existence of material objects."[11] But when Plantinga quotes Calvin in support of this view, he (Calvin) doesn't seem to be saying anything of the sort: Calvin tells us that God "daily discloses himself in the whole workmanship of the universe."[12] He says that even the untutored "cannot be unaware of the excellence of the divine art, for it reveals itself in this innumerable and yet distinct and well-ordered variety of the heavenly host."[13] At first glance it seems extraordinary that such texts can be cited to support the view that Calvin required no evidence for belief in God. Is not "this innumerable and yet distinct and well-ordered variety of the heavenly host" evidence? And does not the notion of divine "workmanship" require previous knowledge that "workmanship" can put beauty and order into things? What can Plantinga mean by saying that Calvin is not appealing to evidence here?--that the prior knowledge cited is not used to *demonstrate strictly* the existence of God? But this seems to be saying only that, in this case, logic is not enough, that insight is needed in addition. Aquinas would agree. To say that the prior knowledge necessary to make such insight possible is not to be called "evidence" seems a quibble.

One can find a basis for this quibble, however, in Calvin's own writing: "To prevent anyone from taking refuge in the pretense of ignorance, God himself has implanted in all men a certain understanding of his divine majesty."[14] Later he adds: "[T]his conviction, namely, that *there is some God*, is naturaly inborn in all . . . ."[15] Like Augustine, Calvin appears to be appealing to the Platonic tradition of "innate ideas" to explain how one comes to know of God's existence. An Aristotelian can happily say that the *capacity for the insight* that there is some God is innate. Calvin apparently prefers to side with Plato and say that what is innate is not merely a capacity for insight, but the very knowledge that there is a God. Plato claimed that innate knowledge needed to be "remembered" and that this remembering had to be triggered by some sort of experience. The lad in the *Meno* has his innate knowledge of geometry triggered by Socrates drawing figures on the ground and asking questions. Perhaps Calvin would prefer to say that our prior knowledge that there is order in the universe and that good workmanship produces order and beauth merely *triggers* our innate idea that God exists; it does not serve as evidence that God exists.

Assuming that this is Calvin's view, let me make two preliminary comments. If, as would appear from these texts, Calvin is primarily concerned to show that those who do not know God are not without fault in this--his purpose could be equally served by appeal to the innate capacity for insight. If people can be held responsible for not having their innate understandings triggered, they can be equally held responsible for not developing their innate capacity for insight. Secondly, while this view of Calvin's is not Aristotelian or Thomistic--it is not original either. Christians who followed Platonic strains of thought (e.g., Augustine and Bonaventure) had long held such views.

Practically speaking, what difference does it make whether one holds the Platonic "innate idea" view or the Aristotelian "insight" view? As long as the only triggering mechanisms considered adequate for "remembering" in the Platonic view are exactly the same as the evidence considered adequate for insight in the Aristotelian view--the practical difference would appear to be slight or non-existent. Both Calvin and Aquinas believe, after all, that the order of the universe can lead even the simple to a notion of God's existence.

Nevertheless, I believe, there are good reasons to prefer the insight view. The connection between "triggering circumstance" and "triggered innate idea" seems far more tenuous--and damagingly so--than that between "evidence" and "evidenced," even when the latter is partly mediated by insight.

Let me use George Mavrodes' story "The Stranger" to illustrate my point.[16] In this story an Indian named Ravi claims that the proposition "Jesus of Nazareth rose from the dead" is self-evident to him. The first time he heard this proposition (from a lapsed Hindu "with no sympathy at all for Christianity")[17] he did not know what "resurrection" meant. Having been informed of the meaning of this word, he immediately found himself believing that Jesus of Nazareth rose from the dead! Ravi says, "I was stuck with the belief and I have been ever since."[18]

Ravi's belief is based on no evidence whatsoever. He knows nothing else about Jesus of Nazareth, about his followers, about his miracles, about his teachings, about the effect of his teachings, or about the sort of testimony given by those who have had faith in him. He just finds himself believing the proposition that he rose from the dead as soon as he understands what it means. Now, this story would appear to fit the "innate idea" model perfectly well--hearing that Jesus rose from the dead triggers Ravi's innate idea to that effect and he finds himself believing it without anything around that even looks as if it could be taken for evidence. It does not fit the "insight" model at all. There is no evidence to serve as a ground for insight. Perhaps the Aristotelian Christian would say that Ravi did not really have Christian faith until he received some further instruction. Before that he simply suffered a strange obsession that was perhaps instrumental in leading him to grounds for genuine faith.

I side with the Aristotelian on this. The evidence in the Scriptures and in the history of the saints is that people do not come to faith in the stark way Ravi is supposed to have done. When we talk about faith, our starting point is the data offered by the coming to faith of actual believers. Ravi's way is just not how it happens. The mere *logical* possibility of such a thing occurring should, it seems to me, interest us no more than the mere *logical* possibility that the earth is flat and carried on the back of a turtle. People come to Christian faith in the presence of testimony, facts, etc., that show the activity of the One in whom they come to believe. An account of coming to faith that gives the role of "evidence" a central place explains these data more satisfactorily, in my opinion, than an account that rules out evidence and then has to place *ad hoc* limits on the triggering mechanisms to show why cases like Ravi's, and even stranger ones, do not actually occur.

What, on the other hand, are the advantages of the "innate idea" approach? Plantinga and Wolterstoff seem convinced that to make acknowledgment of God's existence "basic" is to secure it more solidly for the believer than to base such acknowledgment upon evidence. Why do they think this? As George Mavrodes points out, basic beliefs are not necessarily held with greater conviction than are beliefs based on evidence.[19] Nor are they less subject to revision or replacement. One might add that insights through enlightenment by the Holy Spirit can be of the strongest epistemological sort. The case for "innate ideas" cannot be based upon assumptions about the greater conviction that accompanies basic beliefs. Basic beliefs, as such, may be weak or strong, just as evidenced beliefs are. Why then the decided preference for basicality by Plantinga and Wolerstorff?

Perhaps they think that by making belief in God basic they have an answer for modern skepticism about the evidence of the senses. Perhaps the real reason Plantinga and Wolterstoff insist that belief in God should be understood as basic is not that they think that a basic belief is stronger *per se* than an evidenced belief--but rather because the standard evidence presented for belief in God comes *through the senses* and they believe that such evidence is unreliable because of modern skepticism.

At first it may seem unlikely that Plantinga and Wolterstorff are influenced in this way by modern skepticism. Both seem to believe that our sensory perceptions are to be relied upon. But why do they believe this? Perhaps, like Descartes and Leibniz, they believe this only because of a prior belief in God, a God who cannot deceive and who therefore underwrites the harmony between subject and object that we call knowledge. Descartes and Leibniz claimed to arrive at knowledge of God's existence by "proofs"--while Plantinga and Wolterstorff claim to arrive at it by direct intuition; but all of them claim that the source of such knowledge is ultimately innate.

Now, if *this* is the kind of thinking that motivates Plantinga and Wolterstorff, it clarifies a great deal. Their realism about sense perception is of a distinctly modern sort. It takes modern skepticism seriously and then claims to find a way around it by invoking the divine veracity. The latter is known by direct intuition, not dependent upon the reliability of the senses--thus avoiding circularity. Such preoccupations would explain their strong preference for innate ideas as the basis for belief in God and the strong dissatisfaction with the evidence of the senes as a basis. Nothing else we have discovered appears to explain adequately the strength of these views as held by Plantinga and Wolterstorff.

I do not believe, however, that this way of saving the evidence of the senses works. If one accepts the extravagant arguments for skepticism found in Descartes, Hume, *et al.*, the reasons for continuing in that skepticism, despite the existence of a veracious God, would appear to be no more extravagant. God would know that we have the arguments of Berkeley *et al.* to protect us from gullibility concerning the senses. Why then would it be contrary to the veracity of God for the senses to be radically unreliable as the skeptics insist? God would have given us the wherewithal to protect ourselves to the extent that truth requires, after all. It therefore does not follow from the divine veracity that the senses are radically reliable. What is necessary to overcome sensory skepticism is an *additional* (innate) intuition to the effect that the senses *are* reliable. But then why is this any better than the insight that they are reliable based on sensory experience itself? When one adopts the latter, one denies from the start that modern arguments for sensory skepticism are successful. But, if they are not successful, then the evidence of the senses is not disqualified as an adequate basis for the Spirit-enlightened insights that constitute Christian faith.

To carry the discussion further, I would first have to ask John Calvin, Alvin Plantinga, and other Reformed thinkers who prefer the "innate idea" explanation of faith whether they also invoke innate ideas to solve other epistemological problems, as do Plato and Augustine. If they do, then this discussion must move to a much wider arena than our immediate purposes allow. If some of them do not, however, then I would recommend to them the advantage of not making faith any more discontinuous with other ways of human knowing than is necessary to explain it (to the extent that we can).

In any event, it is clear that John Calvin, Al Plantinga, Nicholas Wolterstorff, and other Reformed thinkers are in good company (Augustine, Bonaventure, and so on) if they choose to invoke "innate ideas." But, in doing so, they do not put forward something new that needs a new name like "Reformed epistemology." They are just following the ancient Platonic and Augustinian line. Nor are they original when they claim "that the propriety or rightness of belief in God in no way depends upon the success or availability of the sort of theistic arguments that form the natural theologian's stock in trade."[20] Plantinga calls this the Reformers' "central insight" on the issue of natural theology. It may well be their central insight, but Aquinas and all other important Christian theologians said as much. Once again there is nothing very distinct here to call "Reformed epistemology." Perhaps *some* Reformed thinkers are more skeptical than Aquinas was of the usefulness of attempting rational proofs for God's existence and nature; but even in this they express the misgivings of an extensive line of predecessors. Nor does the explanation of the widespread human ignorance of God as a result of sin and resistance have its beginning with Reformed Christianity, as Wolterstorff and Mavrodes suggest.[21] This is just the *Christian* explanation held by Paul, Augustine, Bonaventure, Aquinas, and countless others.

To say that John Calvin and Company were less original on these matters than Plantinga and Wolterstorff think is not to find fault with Calvin and Company. On the contrary, they very likely strove to avoid any epistemological discontinuity with their forebears that would have swept themselves entirely outside the pale of Christian faith. They were foundationalists to the core, and they preferred Augustinian (Platonic) forms of foundationalism to Thomistic (Aristotelian) forms. It was not on such issues that they most significantly disagreed with their predecessors in following the Way of Jesus Christ.[22]

E. Faith and Natural Science

In his contribution to *Faith and Rationality*, George Marsden investigates "The Collapse of American Evangelical Academia," that is, the collapse of the Reformed-Evangelical synthesis of science and faith that dominated American intellectual life during most of the 19th century. He argues that, while there were clearly important sociological factors in this collapse (such as increased specialization in American universities), weakness in the Reformed synthesis itself contributed substantially to it and rendered it complete.

The two central flaws of this Reformed-Evangelical synthesis were (1) unstinting enthusiasm for the Baconian pretensions of science; (2) complete confidence in the foundation of all knowledge upon Thomas Reid's notion of "common sense." According to Bacon, the new science was to follow completely reliable procedures from observations to conclusions. There would be no resort to hypothesis--results could be absolutely relied upon. The Evangelicals thought this was just fine. God was not a deceiver, and therefore proper application of the human mind to the facts could not but result in true understanding. And this true understanding would irrefutably reveal the design of God the Creator in the handiwork of nature.

Their complete trust in science seemed to work well for the Evangelicals until science turned its back on religion in the work of Darwin, who explained away design in nature as the result of *chance* mutations, and in the work of Freud, who explained away religion as a symptom of neurosis. Darwin's thesis was the first direct affront. Here science was no longer providing grist for the Evangelical argument from design, but rather undermining it. These Evangelicals had so wrapped themselves in complete trust in science that they were thrown quite off balance by Darwin's theory. Charles Hodge, a prominent Evangelical, tried for a while to deny that Darwin's theories were science at all, claiming that they contradicted common sense, the only sure foundation of science: "But in thus denying design in nature, these writers array against themselves the intuitive perceptions and irresistible convictions of all mankind . . . ."[23] The recognition of design in nature was universal, so Hodge thought, and, being universal, was a matter of "*common*" sense, i.e., was commonly held by all. But this appeal to universal common sense failed the Evangelicals too when it became clear that many people raised on Darwin's theories no longer thought they saw a design in nature requiring a Creator-Designer. The confident symbiosis of religion and science which had served as the foundation of the Evangelical intellectual/academic system seemed irretrievably lost.

Marsden contrasts the intellectual failure of these American Reformed-Evangelicals with what he regards as the success of the *Dutch* Reformed Evangelicals. The Dutch Evangelicals, under the intellectual leadership of Abraham Kuyper, were not so sanguine as their American counterparts about the power of unaided human reason. In this respect they seemed to stay closer to Calvin's emphasis on the sinful condition of the human race. This sinfulness could prevent people of even excellent scientific intelligence from arriving at the knowledge of God. It was possible, in other words, for people most familiar with the order of nature not to recognize in it the hand of God. Given the *dis*ordering effects of human sinfulness, it was possible and even likely that most people and even a vast majority would be unaware of many of the most basic truths that human knowledge is capable of. Kuyper and his Dutch-Reformed brethren, therefore, did not accept universal "common sense" as the criterion of properly basic beliefs. The basic beliefs constituent of Christian faith could thus be grasped by however few without this counting against their truth or justification. Thus armed intellectually, the Dutch-Reformed were able to weather the Darwinian and Freudian affronts with comparative ease, surviving with a vigorous intellectual life intact.

Following Kuyper, Marsden points out that "sinfully determined first principles and commitments can pervade the rest of one's intellectual activity"[24] with the result that one does not recognize or interpret correctly the signs of God. On the other hand, once one has, by the help of the Holy Spirit, adopted the first principles of Christian faith, one sees even the data and conclusions of otherwise secular science in a new light. "Kuyper appears to say something that is almost essential for the survival of the Christian academic community in a secular setting--that science cannot be regarded as a sovereign domain that sets its own rules to which Christians and everyone else must conform if they are to retain their intellectual respectability."[25]

The Thomist finds very little with which to disagree in this analysis of the flaws in the American Evangelical synthesis. Nor does he deny that sinfulness gets in the way of knowledge, inhibiting and preventing it, eclipsing the presence and activity of God. He does not think natural knowledge of God is so impossible as Kuyper seems to think, but he does agree completely that the rich knowledge of God made possible by Revelation is available only by the help of the Holy Spirit.

The Thomist would go on to add some additional points. To adopt Baconian science as one's entire epistemic worldview is mistaken not only because it presents a *part* of human knowledge as though it were the *whole* of it; even the part it presents is presented inaccurately. Not only is the data base allowed by Baconian science too narrow to allow for the full possibilities of human knowledge in, for example, metaphysics, ethics, and religion; but also the type of movement allowed from the data base to larger conclusions is far too restrictive for even the practice of science itself, leaving no room for hypothesis or insight and pretending to accomplish everything by strict demonstration. Baconian science, which was to replace the epistemological idolatries of previous generations, was itself an idol; and the myth of this new idolatry was the myth of strict demonstration.

Descartes, Galileo, Newton, and many others saw their own work as strictly demonstrative. It was fashionable to intersperse one's scientific conclusions with the denial that they were mere "hypotheses." Descartes "demonstrated" that the human heart moves blood through the arteries by heating it to produce a kind of steam pressure.[26] Descartes had no doubt that this was the true explanation of the blood's circulation and that his demonstration was of the foolproof kind mandated by the new method. (God cannot deceive us, after all, when we proceed carefully.) It was fortunate for the Baconian view of science that its most celebrated early case concerned heliocentrism rather than the mechanism of the heart! Galileo's conclusion, following Kepler, happened to be right, Descartes' conclusion happened to be wrong.

Bellarmine was precisely correct when he wrote to Galileo that he (Galileo) had not *demonstrated* heliocentrism, but had only presented a powerful hypothesis. The more exact observations which were needed to definitively rule out Tycho Brahe's geoheliocentric explanation of the data had not yet been made. Newton himself, while eschewing the explicitly metaphysical conjectures of Kepler, did not avoid hypothesis entirely, despite his express intention to do so. The valid range for extrapolation for his very successful laws of motion was no more than hypothesis, given the data he had available. The hypothetical character of the new scientific procedures was recognized by Thomists for what it was. They did not accept the Baconian pretensions of the new science as a body of demonstrated truths.

Meanwhile, most Protestants saw the Galileo case as an opportune embarrassment for the Roman Church and sought to contrast their own acceptance of the new science with the intransigence of the Catholics. This led, in the extreme case, to the full-scale worship of the Baconian idol, taking it as part of true religion, exemplified in the 19th Century American Evangelical thought we have discussed. The ability of Roman Catholicism to withstand the onslaughts of the Darwins and the Freuds was not due simply to its "strongly institutionalized authority" (the usual Protestant analysis repeated by Marsden),[27] but due much more to its philosophical/theological ability to locate the hypothetical procedures of the new science within a wider context of method and knowledge. Some Catholics argued that no amount of "scientific method" could produce more than instrumentally successful conjecture. Others, more ironically, conceded that the method might occasionally produce a theory so well and completely confirmed as to make a strong claim to be true. In practice, scientists clearly were *striving* for the knowledge of *true causes*, but the immense difficulty of the task often thwarted even their most brilliant efforts, as theory succeeded theory.

Darwin's hypotheses concerning the origins of species, which caused so much trouble for American Evangelicals, illustrate the point. Darwin's model for evolution called for constant mutation, resulting in *gradual* variation *within* species, accumulating over a long time into the development of *new* species. The fossil record has never supported this model. Rather, even in Darwin's time, the fossil record showed protracted periods of complete stability within species, followed by the relatively sudden emergence of new species, often accompanied by the decline or elimination of older ones. The emergence of new species was so sudden that, assuming evolution to be its cause, there was not enough time for a fossil record of the intervening mutations to be set down. Only recently have evolutionary biologists been willing to admit the impact of their own data: today a theory of "periodic" evolution has all but supplanted that of "gradual" evolution. Not only was Darwin's theory hypothetical, at a very key point it simply walked roughshod over its own data. Furthermore, this fact was practically ignored for decades by the biology establishment.

Mutations by mere *chance* seem less plausible as an explanation for dramatic, periodic evolution than as an explanation for very slow, gradual evolution. And the evidence for even periodic evolution is much weaker than had long been assumed for species evolution in general.

An argument from Design is surely not necessary to justify Christian faith, but Darwin's hypotheses are less a threat to such reasoning, for those who care to use it, than has been assumed by most 20th century intellectuals. Indeed, the case can be made that it was precisely in order to forestall such "design reasoning" on the part of the religious that early Darwinian apologists, such as Huxley, slanted their premises as far as possible to support *chance* as the explanatory cipher. This extrinsic motivation, in order to secure the conciousness of the intelligentsia on the side of Darwinian evolution, illustrates how unreliable such mass consciousness can be as a basis for universal common sense taken as the foundation of knowledge. The mass consciousness of the intellectual elite has for many decades now been arrayed against religious faith; and only those Christians--Reformed, Catholic, or whatever--who know why they are unimpressed by its pretensions, have been able to resist it intelligently.

Center for Thomistic Studies

NOTES

1. Nicholas Wolterstorff, "Introduction," *FR*, 9.

2. *FR*, 4.

3. *FR*, 4-5.

4. Alvin Plantinga, "Reason and Belief in God," *FR*, 44.

5. Thomas Aquinas, *De Veritate*, q. 14, a. 10, cited by Plantinga, *FR*, 44.

6. *FR*, 47.

7. Thomas Aquinas, *Summa Contra Gentiles*, III, 38, cited by Plantinga, *FR*, 47.

8. *FR*, 47.

9. *FR*, 60.

10. *FR*, 47.

11. *FR*, 17 (emphasis added).

12. John Calvin as cited by Plantinga, *FR*, 66.

13. *FR*, 66.

14. *FR*, 65.

15. *FR*, 66.

16. George I. Mavrodes, "The Stranger," *FR*, 94-102.

17. *FR*, 100.

18. Ibid.

19. George I. Mavrodes, "Jerusalem and Athens Revisited," *FR*, 214-216.

20. Plantinga, *FR*, 72.

21. Mavrodes, *FR*, 202.

22. For my more general argument in favor of the Aristotelian sort of epistemological foundationalism, see my *Prospectus for the Triumph of Realism* (Macon, GA: Mercer University Press, 1987).

23. George Marsden, "The Collapse of American Evangelical Academia," *FR*, 244.

24. *FR*, 256.

25. *FR*, 255.

26. René Descartes, *Discourse on Method*, Part V.

27. Marsden, "The Collapse of American Evangelical Academia," *FR*, 220.

OTHER PUBLICATIONS OF
THE CENTER FOR THOMISTIC STUDIES

100 Years of Thomism
Victor B. Brezik, C.S.B., ed.

Articles by Henry Veatch, Vernon Bourke, James Weisheipl,
Victor Brezik, Anton Pegis, and Joseph Owens.

Thomistic Papers I
Victor B. Brezik, C.S.B., ed.

Articles by Henry Veatch, Vernon Bourke, James Weisheipl,
Victor Brezik, Anton Pegis, and Joseph Owens.

Thomistic Papers II
Leonard A. Kennedy, C.S.B., and Jack C. Marler, eds.

*Articles by Laurence Shook, Desmond FitzGerald, Robert Henle,
Francis Kovach, Joseph Owens, and Frederick Wilhelmsen.*

Thomistic Papers III
Leonard A. Kennedy, C.S.B., ed.

Articles by Joseph Owens, Edward Synan, Benedict Ashley,
Bernard Doering, and Gerry Lessard.

Wisdom from St. Augustine
Vernon J. Bourke

Fourteen very readable articles gathered from many periodicals.

About Beauty: A Thomistic Interpretation
Armand A. Maurer, C.S.B.

An Interpretation of Existence
Joseph Owens, C.Ss.R.

An Elementary Christian Metaphysics
Joseph Owens, C.Ss.R.

A Catalogue of Thomists, 1270-1900
Leonard A. Kennedy, C.S.B.

The names and works of over 2,000 writers with a Thomist reputation, arranged by century, country, and (where applicable) religious community.

Known From the Things that Are
Fundamental Theory of the Moral Life
Martin D. O'Keefe, S.J.

A theoretical and applied treatment of ethics. The argumentation throughout is philosophical, and no conclusions contradict the teaching of the Church's Magisterium.

Substance and Modern Science
Richard J. Connell

Avoiding traditional philosophical terminology, this book shows how the notion of substance is valid in modern chemistry, physics, and biology.

All publications of the Center should be ordered from:

University of Notre Dame Press
Notre Dame, Indiana 46556

This book was
Wordprocessed by Sister Terese Auer, O.S.F.
Formatted by Joanne Knasas
And laserprinted by:

Desktop Publishing Center
5001 Bissonnet, Suite 101
Bellaire, Texas 77401